To O's Book Club,
We Need Diverse Books,
#OwnVoiceBooks,
and to all of the movements that
remind students and teachers alike
of the joys of reading.

SONJA CHERRY-PAUL | DANA JOHANSEN

Foreword by Cornelius Minor

Breathing New Life into
Book Clubs

A PRACTICAL GUIDE FOR TEACHERS

HEINEMANN
Portsmouth, NH

Heinemann
361 Hanover Street
Portsmouth, NH 03801–3912
www.heinemann.com

Offices and agents throughout the world

Library of Congress Cataloging-in-Publication Data
Names: Cherry-Paul, Sonja, author. | Johansen, Dana, author.
Title: Breathing new life into book clubs : a practical guide for teachers / Sonja Cherry-Paul, Dana Johansen.
Description: Portsmouth, NH : Heinemann Publishing, [2019] | Foreword / Cornelius Minor Gratitude—Creating a culture of reading through book clubs—Organizing and setting up book clubs—Launching and managing book clubs—Lighting the fire of discussion—Resources at a glance— Living with books all year long. | Includes bibliographical references.
Identifiers: LCCN 2019009415 | ISBN 9780325076850
Subjects: LCSH: Reading (Elementary) | Reading (Middle school) | Book clubs (Discussion groups)

Classification: LCC LB1573 .C447 2019 | DDC 372.4—dc23
LC record available at https://lccn.loc.gov/2019009415

Editor: *Holly Kim Price*
Production: *Hilary Goff*
Cover and interior designs: *Suzanne Heiser*
Typesetter: *Shawn Girsberger*
Manufacturing: *Steve Bernier*

Printed in the United States of America on acid-free paper
23   22   21   20   VP   3   4   5

February 2020

Contents

To download and
print digital versions of the
reproducible forms found in this book,
visit the online resources at
http://hein.pub/newlifebookclubs-login.
Enter your email address and password
(or click "Create New Account" to set up an account).
Once you have logged in, enter keycode
NULIFE
and click "Register."

Foreword

by Cornelius Minor

When I was a kid, I used to love it when my aunts came over for my mom's book club gatherings. They would come by the carload. This group of radiant women would enter the house and fill it with warmth. And food. And laughter. And hugs. And brilliance. And stories. And the kind of grown-folks' talk that kids like me always wanted to hear, but could never understand.

I would hide out at the top of the stairs—long after I had been sent to bed—straining my ears to pluck a phrase or a sentence from the affable, brainy cacophony of sound emitted by my aunts and their books in the dining room below me. If I was lucky, I would catch the recitation of an entire passage of text or the telling of a deeply personal anecdote.

If you know Liberian women, you know that these women were not my aunts by blood or by marriage. They were my aunts because they went to college, attended church, shared offices, endured husbands, and navigated life with my mother. They were my aunts because when they occupied the same space as my mom, worries were shed, challenges were overcome, and doubts were erased.

Those stolen moments at the top of the stairs were my early introduction to the reality that my mom—the spiritual and physical center of my family—was not just a caregiver, problem-solver, or juice-box purveyor. She is beautifully and completely human. Similarly, children are not levels or behaviors or the complicated pasts that sometimes follow them into our classrooms. We do not group them to keep them quiet. And quiet does not mean "good." Each young person that we serve is beautifully and completely human. Dana and Sonja know this.

They teach us what years of eavesdropping on my aunts taught me—that book clubs are not merely about books and discussion protocols. They are about the humans that come to them, the people that we become when we are in them, and the powerful people that endure—long after we put the texts down—because we have read together.

Book clubs are not quiet. They are not passive. They are not about filling in the blanks, answering the question, or being the "recorder" or "discussion leader." Book clubs are about finding meaning in texts and finding community in others. Dana and Sonja know this.

Though I did not have the words for it at the time, I loved seeing my mother come to life around my aunts. When they came over to talk, my mom seemed taller, happier, *more alive.* This is what book clubs do. **They make us more alive.**

Dana and Sonja's work is powerful because beyond guiding us into the structures, routines, and lessons that ensure meaningful reading and purposeful talk, they expertly guide us toward crafting the experiences that give children multiple opportunities to live as readers, as thinkers, and as members of a community. Dana and Sonja understand that whenever our society has been confronted with big questions, well-read young people have always been the answer.

The Declaration of Independence was written by well-read young people. Well-read young people fought and won the right to vote for women and African Americans. Well-read young people founded the NAACP, GLSEN, and many of the organizations that force us to examine what we mean when we say freedom for all people or education for all children.

Though adults consistently fail to act on gun control, climate change, healthcare, or income inequality, well-read young people continue to speak out. On every issue, they are present. In a world that has not learned to listen properly when kids speak, Dana and Sonja teach us how to give kids the tools and supports to keep reading, thinking, and talking anyway. They know that kids who read powerfully, think critically, and listen empathetically to each other will change the world. Just like the generations of well-read kids before them.

Gratitude

From Dana and Sonja:

It is a privilege to be part of the Heinemann family. Thank you to our incredible editor, Holly Kim Price, for all of the ways you encouraged us to take risks throughout the writing process, and for your unwavering support for this project. Also, many thanks to Vicki Boyd, Kim Cahill, Sherry Day, Michelle Flynn, Sarah Fournier, Anita Gildea, Hilary Goff, Michael Grover, Suzanne Heiser, Krysten Lebel, Roderick Spelman, and Brett Whitmarsh. We are convinced that you possess a dash of magic mixed with remarkable talent, dedication, and hard work. A special thank you to Ken Lundberg and students at Pollard Middle School!

From Dana:

Having reading role models is one of the most treasured gifts we can have in our lives. I want to thank the reading role models in my life who have taught me how to read with joy and curiosity. This book would not exist without your love and support. To my mom who has always been in book clubs and always "read by example." To my dad who carried stacks of Rainbow Brite and Cabbage Patch Kids books to read aloud on our train ride commutes each weekend. Thank you both for the joyful reading memories. Thank you, also, to my family: Steve, Kathy, Bonnie, Erin, and Nick for all your support and love.

Thank you to Lucy Calkins for your support and guidance throughout my journey as a writer. You changed my life the day you said, "I'd like to introduce you to my editor at Heinemann." I will always be grateful. And to Cornelius Minor: you are an inspiration to me, and one of the most generous spirits I have ever met. Thank you for sharing your passion for teaching reading and writing. You are a one-of-a-kind teacher, and I am overjoyed that you said "Yes!" to helping us with our project.

A huge thank-you to Molly King, Mark Feiner, Becky Walker, and the entire Greenwich Academy community! Thank you also to Mere Tormey, Jenny Collins, and the entire Group V team: Meagan Jones, Kate Lee, Sarah Popescu, and Doug Rendell. I feel so blessed to be able to work with an incredible group of colleagues who inspire me each day. To Jeanette Tyndall, thank you for encouraging me to pursue my studies in literacy and packing my professional library with must-reads. To Ugina Covington, thank you for teaching me the joy of children's literature. To JoAnne Vicidomini, thank you for first introducing me to book clubs! I am forever grateful. To Melissa Wilson, my partner for eight years of fourth-grade book clubs: you taught me the importance of the book club calendar, student choice, and reading with joy. A big thank you to Joanne Marciano and Tara Lencl, my incredible writing group! And to my colleagues Maureen Corbo, Mariana Keels, Jeff Schwartz, Stephanie Seidel, and Joan Slattery—a *huge* thank-you for sharing your wisdom within the pages of this text. I am so honored to have you with me on this journey. And, of course, my writing life would not be the same without the support of Connie Blunden and Julie FitzPatrick. Thank you both so much for always keeping me grounded with a glass of wine and great discussion. To all my students, past and present: My wish for you is that you lead a life of joyful reading. Never stop being curious and always share your love of reading with others. You are my inspiration each day and my greatest reading role models.

And lastly, a heartfelt thank-you to Sonja Cherry-Paul. You are my writing partner, my friend, my family. What a journey the last ten years have been! Through all the ups and downs, you have been my rock. Together, we've shared many joy-filled memories, and I cannot imagine my journey without you. Here's to all the laughter we've yet to laugh!

From Sonja:

This year has led to both remarkable personal and professional revelations. It has been a year of facing tremendous challenges and walking toward light. I am grateful to so many people who, throughout this process, have enveloped me in warmth. In immeasurable ways, your support enabled this book to take form.

Frank, you are the sun, my compass. If I am strong, it is because of the restorative power of your love. Imani, you are the light. My whole world brightens at the sound of your voice.

Thanks to my parents, Edward and Mary, and my brother Eddie for your love and encouragement. I am incredibly grateful to all of my family, and particularly to Jason, Nikki, Ella, and Nina for providing me with the most epic writing breaks any writer could dream of.

I am deeply grateful to Lucy Calkins. You have been a steady beam of light. More than once, and in various contexts, you've helped me to find my way.

I am so thankful for Karen Hammerness and Tom Hatch and the numerous ways you've sustained and encouraged me.

It is an honor to have such a brilliant, talented circle of educators who open my eyes and challenge me: Sara Ahmed, Colleen Cruz, Carolyn Denton, Tricia Ebarvia, Erica Finegan, Melissa Garcia, Catherine Gigantino, Abbe Hocherman, Jodi Honeycutt, Aeriale Johnson, Danielle LaBella, Tara Lencl, Dr. Joanne Marciano, Jackie Marcus, Jenice Mateo-Toledo, Anna Osborn, Dr. Kim Parker, Jocelyn Perez, Tiana Silvas, Erica Williams, Michelle Yang-Kaczmarek. As much as I admire you and am grateful to know you professionally, I am also so fortunate to call you my friends.

To Cornelius Minor, as I always say, there's nothing "minor" about the way you have indelibly influenced the lives of so many educators and students. I am grateful to call you my friend as well.

And finally, but foremost, to Dana Johansen. I'm forever grateful that we found each other outside of Grace Dodge Hall, thirty minutes before the first night of our first graduate class. This encounter has changed the course of my life. It's been a journey ever since, and I'm so glad to be on it with you.

1: Creating a Culture of Reading Through Book Clubs

> *My advice to teachers is to give your students as much freedom as possible in book clubs.*
>
> —MIA, FIFTH-GRADE STUDENT

When you think of an adult book club, what images come to mind? Chances are you're picturing a comfortable space such as your home or that of another club member. Perhaps the gatherings are at a quaint café or in a beloved restaurant. You might know the members of your club as your close friends or colleagues. Or possibly the club members are from a Meetup that you've just joined, and you are interested in getting to know some new people. You might also picture food (savory or sweet bites of something prepared just for the occasion) and continuous drinks (coffee, tea, wine). And in this comfortable space, the conversation is fluid. At times some members turn to another close by to share something that may or may not be spoken out loud to the entire group. Discussions fluctuate from the beginning of the book to the end in no particular order; between statements and questions, and characters and setting. There are agreements about ideas as well as disagreements that result in spirited conversations. Finally, a hallmark of an adult book club is that it is a place where the members completely lose track of time.

𝄞 A Vision for Book Clubs

When we picture book clubs in our classrooms, we envision many of the same wonderful components of adult book clubs. We imagine small groups clustered together in cozy spots around our room. Perhaps they are seated on the carpet, at a table, or at a group of desks. Some may be gathered beneath their club banner or in a makeshift cardboard clubhouse. In our mind's eye, we see our students making reading plans with their club, talking about books, and asking each other questions. In this hum of activity, we hear joyful laughter and see new friendships created. We feel the positive energy in the classroom as clubs meet. We picture our students engaging in the same adult experience that we admire, and we feel proud of our students' level of preparedness and their eagerness to take part in their club's discussion.

As we imagine book clubs in our classrooms, we envision our students doing the work we've been teaching. They are putting their learning into action.

Some groups of students talk in an animated manner as they set reading goals and cheer each other on. We hear words of encouragement such as, "We can do this! Let's read twenty pages tonight and make five sticky notes." Our students are in charge of their reading lives, and they feel empowered to challenge themselves as readers and work collaboratively as a team.

While we dream of having book clubs in our classrooms that provide the joyful experience of adult book clubs, we've also found that there can be hiccups. Sometimes our clubs are roaring successes, and at other times, the clubs fizzle and fall apart. Over the years we've heard from fellow educators who have faced similar challenges with book clubs. "They're too complicated to manage." "Are the kids really reading?" "Are their discussions really deepening their understanding of the text?" We've also heard from teachers who've never tried book clubs because of their worries about time and rigor. "I don't have time for this!" "What do I teach in book clubs?" "Are my students just doing their own thing?" "How do I assess their understanding of the book?"

We admit it. We've experienced frustration ourselves. We've come close to throwing in the towel when it comes to book clubs. Stepping back to examine all of our concerns, a common theme emerges: a fear of letting go. Although we want our students to have control over their reading, we have concerns. As teachers, it's our job to make sure that all of our students are learning and growing, and it's easier for us to imagine this happening underneath our watchful eyes where we can anticipate pitfalls and plan pathways for success. Sometimes it's challenging for us to imagine that, independently, our students will make the best decisions about their reading. We worry that they will not hold themselves accountable; have on-task, meaningful conversations about texts with their peers; and take the clubs seriously. The truth is that we can't always re-create our image of the ideal adult book club in our classrooms. For instance, not all club members will keep up with the reading. During conversations, some members will get off topic. Some voices will be louder than others, and others may not speak at all. At times, club meetings may seem like total chaos! Although we may worry about giving up control to our students, there are ways we can avoid and repair these challenges.

Over the past twenty years of teaching students in elementary and middle school, we've tried many approaches to teaching readers—whole-class texts, leveled reading groups, literature circles, and independent reading. We've experienced successes and failures in all aspects of our teaching. However, over the course of our teaching journey, we've kept one piece constant—we've always had book clubs. The reason is simple: to nurture students' love of reading and their desire to share the experience with others. Despite our hectic daily lives, adults join book clubs. We are exhausted at the end of the workday. The gym (or the sofa!) beckons. There are errands to run and children to pick up from soccer practice. Yet, we make time for book clubs. We join book clubs because we long to be part of communities of readers. Books, friends, and thoughtful, rich conversations. And isn't this passion for reading exactly what we want for our students? A space where they share ideas, take risks, and nurture a culture of reading? Book clubs create close-knit communities of readers and thinkers and help students become lifelong readers.

To be honest, our vision for book clubs continues to be a work in progress. It is informed by our own experiences and our ongoing dialogue with fellow educators, as well as our research. Together, this has become the fountain of knowledge that we draw upon. And we'd like to share our vision with you. No matter your reading curricula, we'd like to show you *why* book clubs should become an essential part of your school year and *how* to make that happen. Whether you're looking to breathe new life into book clubs or begin implementing them in your classroom, we invite you to join us on this journey.

Becoming a Nation of Lifelong Readers

While thinking about the value of book clubs, we began by asking ourselves: Are we a nation of lifelong readers? The answer is complex. To address this question, we looked at how students feel about reading, as well as how they are performing in reading in the United States. "To Read or Not to Read: A Question of National Consequence" (National Endowment for the Arts 2007) offers statistical data on the nation's reading trends, and the results are alarming. According to this 2007 report, Americans were reading less. Only 33 percent of thirteen-year-olds read daily, and 19 percent of seventeen-year-olds did not or rarely read for pleasure at all. And yet, for 65 percent of seventeen-year-old students, the amount of reading done for school or homework remained constant from data gathered as early as 1992—about fifteen pages per day or fewer. The National Assessment of Educational Progress (NAEP) assesses the reading performance of fourth, eighth, and twelfth graders in both public and private schools across the country. The results are compiled by the National Center for Education Statistics (NCES). In 2015, eighth-grade reading performance scores decreased from 2013. And by twelfth grade, students reading at or above the basic performance level was slightly lower in 2015 than 2013. The 2017 results published in April 2018 demonstrate little change in the average reading performance assessments for fourth and eighth graders.

The ubiquity of technology and the impact this has on children's lives adds further complexity to whether or not we are a nation of lifelong readers. In 2017, CNN (Howard 2017) and NPR (Kamenetz 2017) reported that children are spending more time in front of screens. Children eight years old and younger spend more time on screens (about forty-eight minutes each day) than reading or being read to (about thirty minutes per day). These data demonstrate what James Steyer, CEO and founder of Common Sense Media, calls "a seismic shift" that is "fundamentally redefining childhood experiences" (Kamenetz 2017). He asserts that the nation is just beginning to understand the implications of this. As both reading and blended-learning educators, we are concerned about these data. With our students busy after-school lives being packed with sports practice, music lessons, and more, combined with hours each day exploring social media, playing video games, and watching television, how are kids finding time to read? According to the research, it seems, quite possibly, that they aren't. These results imply that when it comes to our students, additional work is needed to become the nation of readers we hope to be.

Adolescence is a critical time for reading. Although it may be challenging for educators to affect the reading lives and identities of nine- and ten-year-olds, it can be even more difficult to develop the reading identities of middle and high school students. This, however, is not a new challenge. Nancie Atwell addressed this phenomenon in her book *In the Middle.* She writes, "Reading necessarily takes a back seat as teenagers' worlds become impossibly full. . . . When reading doesn't happen at school, it's unlikely to happen away from school, which means it's unlikely to happen at all" [1987, 156]. To transform the reading lives of our students, educators will need to consider the ways we value and make space for reading in our classrooms.

Research has helped educators gain both general and nuanced understandings about the teaching of reading. Such research has informed reading instruction in terms of the best practices to strengthen students' skills, document reading gains, and improve reading attitudes. However, there have been tensions and contradictions in the field around reading instruction over the decades. Some of the misunderstandings are perhaps a result of lack of awareness of important reading research findings. For example, researchers have found that when an emphasis is placed on the volume of reading in literacy curricula, through independent reading, students' reading fluency and comprehension improves. Richard Allington argues, "There is a potent relationship between volume of reading and reading achievement" [2012, 53]. When kids read more, there is an increase in reading achievement. Lucy Calkins urges, "The single most important thing we can do to turn schools around, making them into places where youngsters thrive as readers, is to clear out the time and space so that children can learn to read by reading" [2010, 7]. One way for students to make gains in reading achievement and become the lifelong readers we desire them to be is through book clubs.

We have mapped the research field and, in Figure 1.1, have summarized six major findings that highlight what is important about book clubs and how students benefit from them.

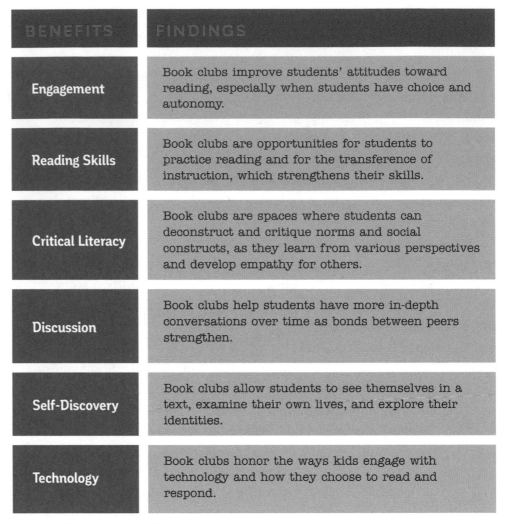

BENEFITS	FINDINGS
Engagement	Book clubs improve students' attitudes toward reading, especially when students have choice and autonomy.
Reading Skills	Book clubs are opportunities for students to practice reading and for the transference of instruction, which strengthens their skills.
Critical Literacy	Book clubs are spaces where students can deconstruct and critique norms and social constructs, as they learn from various perspectives and develop empathy for others.
Discussion	Book clubs help students have more in-depth conversations over time as bonds between peers strengthen.
Self-Discovery	Book clubs allow students to see themselves in a text, examine their own lives, and explore their identities.
Technology	Book clubs honor the ways kids engage with technology and how they choose to read and respond.

Figure 1.1 The Benefits of Book Clubs

As a result of our research, three major points jumped out at us. First, several terms have been used interchangeably with the phrase *book clubs*. These include: literature circles, book groups, reading clubs, learning clubs, and literature study groups. For some educators, there are nuances between each of these terms, and for others there may not be. We like *book clubs* best because, frankly, it's kid friendly. Second, the research emphasizes two defining principles of a book club: choice and ownership. Students in a book club must have autonomy and the power to choose what they read. Therefore, we define a book club as a space where a specific group of individuals meet physically and/or virtually for a fixed period of time for the purpose of reading and discussing a self-selected text. Third, although strengthening students' skills is paramount to teachers, particularly as we educate children in a standards-driven era, the research shows that the benefits of book clubs extend far beyond reading com-

prehension. We value book clubs because of their indelible influence on students as they develop as critical thinkers, lifelong readers, and change makers in the world.

Creating a Culture of Reading

How did Oprah Winfrey get America excited about reading? She formed a book club. Perhaps you too were a member. From 1996 until present, Oprah's Book Club is the biggest and most successful book club the world has ever seen! In essence, she changed the culture of reading in our country by changing *what* and *how* we read. As a result, millions of people discovered, or rekindled, a passion for reading. Libraries are frequented by readers who want to borrow a copy of the latest "O" book they've placed on hold. Books sales have catapulted to the delight of booksellers and authors. It is as if the entire nation has been under a potent, pleasurable spell that compels it to read, read, read! It is also one of our first models of a digital book club as members connect with one another around the nation and beyond. From 1996 to 2002, not only could we view Oprah, our reading guru, on television with the author of the O book of the month, guiding us through the richness the book has to offer, we could also participate in global conversations with members through digital platforms we could access from our kitchen tables or from bed. And we continue to participate in O's Book Club digitally today.

But how did Oprah accomplish this? She did so by creating a culture for reading through book clubs. Culture is how people connect and come to understand each other better. When we help students to nurture a culture for reading in their book clubs, they will delve into the stories of others and realize that they are their own. Book clubs break the barriers of isolationism. They inspire students to examine their lives as well as think about others different from themselves.

Book clubs are where students fall in love with reading, but we value book clubs because it is in these spaces that we witness humanity at its best. Through the process of reading and responding to texts, students come to understand each other better. They reflect on who they are, where they hope to be, and the ties that bind them together. The attitudes, traditions, values, and goals established in book clubs often become the principles that guide the way students live their lives. As such, we can invite students to record the story of their book club in a journal or on a blog—the laughs, the struggles, the triumphs, and the lessons learned that will stay with them.

Essential Components for Book Clubs

As a result of reading the research and speaking with numerous educators of grades 3–12, we believe the following components are the seeds of success that can be sowed in the book clubs we nurture in our classrooms. These are the components we believe are essential to creating, maintaining, and sustaining book clubs: conversation, reading time, technology, written responses, observing, coaching, and assessment. These components are not linear, but circuitous and interconnected. They may not all be enacted daily but will occur over the life span of a book club. In Figure 1.2 you will see the essential components.

Figure 1.2 Essential Components for Book Clubs

These components delineate what the teachers and students are doing during the book club meeting times. Distinct yet overlapping features of book club meetings enable educators to clearly discern what is happening during club meetings. It helps to think about the process of making book clubs function successfully as a Ferris wheel. You can see in your mind a joyful experience filled with friends and laughter. The wheel is a circle of interconnected pieces that go around and around, and at the center of the wheel is the hub. Next, we unpack the features of the components to make clear the importance of each part and how they work together.

DISCUSSION

For book clubs, the hub is the discussion. It is the reason we form clubs, and it is the social spark that ignites students' enthusiasm for reading. Whether it is talking about the text, asking questions, or making reading goals, discussion is at the heart of every book club meeting. All spokes of the wheel feed into the hub, and when they work together, the conversation is superb. We are able to see transference and application of the reading strategies we've been teaching, and we see our students take ownership of their reading lives. Therefore, it is important and necessary to broaden our conception of what discussion looks like. For some it may be a quieter time and for others a more boisterous time. We also appreciate the many ways that technology aids our understanding of a discussion, and we know that digital tools can allow our students to have powerful exchanges.

PLANNING

Planning is critical for the success of book clubs. For some clubs, this may happen at the beginning of the meeting. For some, it occurs at the end. And for others, it may be happening all throughout the entire meeting. But one of the ways we help book clubs run efficiently is by helping students understand the importance of planning. When clubs plan, they ask and address many questions such as: What will we accomplish today? How will we use our time? Are we meeting our reading goals? How can we improve our discussions? Should we use technology to assist our work and how? How much should we read before our next meeting? What can we do to have more fun in our clubs? An essential component to planning is reflection. For clubs to move forward to achieve their goals involves students looking back and determining what's working well and what they must alter. Although planning may look different in each book club and even from day to day, the common components include goal setting, time management, and reflection.

READING

Also integral to a strong club meeting is reading time. We are fierce advocates of independent reading time each day, and we believe it is equally important for students to have the opportunity to read with each other during book club meetings. It's not necessary for students to read together at every meeting. However, it is important to encourage your students to read passages of the text together. This meaningful experience allows students to share their personal reactions to the text. They will ooh and aah! Reading together is one of the ways that book clubs motivate readers and create a community. When students read together, you will observe their reading skills in action. You will see students summarize portions of the text together, check for each other's understanding, and ask questions. When students read together, they model good reading habits for each other.

DIGITAL TOOLS

Technology gives educators the tools they need to create digital spaces for reading response and discussion. When we think of discussion as the hub, we imagine a spoke of the wheel as the technology that helps all voices be heard in the club. Digital tools such as Padlet, Kidblog, Flipgrid, and Word-Press help teachers create blogs and message boards for students to share their ideas. Just as Nerdy Book Club and O's Book Club play a role in our adult book club lives, creating spaces like these enables our students to connect to each other, other classes, and the world.

WRITTEN RESPONSE

Another key component of book clubs is written response. Students' written responses about the text might look like sticky notes, written journal entries, reflections, or blog posts. Although adult book clubs do not make writing mandatory, some members will jot notes in the margins, on the last page of the novel, or on paper. It's often quite interesting to see all the many ways that adults record their thoughts and musings, and it's equally important to offer our students a variety of ways to respond to a text that feel authentic to them. The ways students respond may change from text to text and even throughout the duration of book clubs. We also appreciate how Lucy Calkins has helped teachers rethink lengthy reading written responses and how this can impede the reading we want our students to do. Book clubs especially are not the time to request essays and reports, but instead the time to expect concise, powerful bursts of expression that demonstrate students' understanding and insights.

OBSERVATION

Equally important as the work that students are doing during book club meetings is that of the teachers. Observation plays a key role in book clubs, as the teacher moves around the room listening to the clubs' discussions. The process of observing is sensory based and goes beyond

what we can see, and it includes what we hear, and the feeling we're getting about interpersonal relationships within clubs. This involves paying keen attention to the verbal and nonverbal cues that help us to determine: What does it feel like to be in this club? Are each of the members thriving? During this time, we are also observing our students' reading strategies in action, and we are making notes about what we are noticing. These notes become the artifacts we collect to springboard the coaching we'll do with a particular club. For instance, we may note that in one club, our students are having difficulty using setting details to inform their thinking about a character's actions. In another group, we may notice that students are reluctant to speak up when they disagree with an idea being discussed. Heightening our awareness of what's really happening in book clubs involves teachers becoming researchers. And we know that the best research begins with observation.

COACHING

Not only is every teacher a teacher of reading and writing, but every teacher is a coach. In many schools, we are grateful for literacy coaches who keep us up-to-date with everything from learning standards to current teaching strategies to new resources. But when we think about the word *coach*, the context that most frequently comes to mind is often sports. Whether it's softball, basketball, or soccer, teachers can apply the techniques of these coaches to the type of coaching students need in book clubs. There's practice time, when players exercise to increase stamina, coaches review the plays and provide pointers, and players practice the plays applying feedback from the coach. However, once the game is happening, the time designated for practice simply doesn't exist. The coach can address the team throughout the game, but this happens in the course of minutes, because the players have to get back to the game. Think about book clubs as "the game" and it's happening . . . now! Extended, multilayered lessons have no place during book clubs. Reserve such direct teaching for another time in your reading instruction. Instead, aim to provide a quick strategy or suggestion, and it should take teachers five minutes or less to do so. In short, unless a club is in crisis, we should get in and get out and let students do the work of readers of and respondents to texts.

ASSESSMENT

Good teaching begins with an initial idea of what you are going to assess. This backward design allows us to map the skills we hope our students will learn by the end of a unit or lesson. In this way, book clubs are no different from any other unit you teach. Since the clubs are run by your students, and you are acting as an observer and a coach, it can feel as though you do not have concrete assessments to identify your students' learning. We've experienced this feeling in book clubs. However, we have highlighted specific observational and written response strategies that will help you assess the learning that is happening during book clubs, so you know that your students are making progress as readers.

So Why This Book?

As full-time teachers ourselves, we've yearned for a book that pulls together the research and best practices that help us have the "best book clubs ever"! And although we found pieces of the puzzle in various places, we couldn't help but notice an important gap: there simply wasn't a book that exclusively addressed the nuts and bolts of book clubs—how to create, maintain, and sustain them. So we decided to create this resource for ourselves and for other educators. Furthermore, as blended-learning educators, we desire to instruct using educational, sound methods that infuse technology. Therefore, a blended-learning book club approach is one that we are excited to share with educators who also care about their students accessing technology in authentic, meaningful ways in literacy instruction.

The research statistics we've discussed show we are at a crossroads when it comes to our students and reading. However, we cannot give up. We cannot allow the dip in unmotivated readers to grow. In the years to come we want to see a rise in the number of readers who are excited to read for pleasure. We want our students to be passionate about reading. How do we fight against the wave of distractions and new technology that flood our students' lives? How do we win what may appear to be a losing battle? We act boldly and bravely, and we adjust. We breathe new life into what we're doing. We change with the times, and we seek to disrupt the status quo. We start a reading revolution. To truly become a nation of lifelong readers, we must create a culture of reading in our classrooms. We believe this can be accomplished through book clubs, where students have autonomy and are empowered to read and respond in ways that are authentic and meaningful to them.

In addition to reflecting on the current reading research, we amplify the voices of teachers and students from various grade levels to provide the honest truth about book clubs. Chapters 3, 4, and 5 include minilessons that address common pitfalls you and your students may experience, along with pathways that can help you to overcome these hurdles. Chapter 6 includes resources to help students commemorate book club experiences. Although there is no one right way to approach book clubs, and no universal panacea to solve the issues that will inevitably arise, we hope our book will inspire you to join us on this journey to breathe new life into book clubs. Here's how the journey will continue to unfold:

Chapter 2—Organizing and Setting Up Book Clubs

There are several logistics involved in planning for book clubs. Where do I get the books? What types of clubs can I offer? How will I group my students?

Chapter 3—Launching and Managing Book Clubs

Ensuring that book clubs run smoothly from start to finish requires several key minilessons. How do I fit book clubs into the curriculum? What do students do during book club meetings? What is my role as the teacher?

Chapter 4—Lighting the Fire of Discussion

Book clubs are energetic, loud, productive spaces. How can I honor the authentic ways kids communicate without fear that discussions will run amok? Which methods help students to flourish as discussants of texts and of their ideas?

Chapter 5—Journeying Through Texts with Peers

Reading comprehension strategies help students journey through texts together. How can I teach students to navigate fiction and nonfiction texts in their book clubs? What scaffolding do students need to live confidently within the pages of a text? Which methods help students to dive deep into a text to make discoveries about themselves and the world?

Chapter 6—Living with Books All Year Long

Culminating activities are opportunities for students to celebrate their club's achievements. How can I create meaningful and exciting ways to wrap up book club journeys? How can I provide pathways for book club experiences beyond our classroom doors?

2: Organizing and Setting Up Book Clubs

When it comes to reading, engagement is everything. Book clubs engage our readers. Our students feed on positive peer energy to challenge themselves to read more and say more. In book clubs, students work together to make sense of a text, and from this experience they learn. So how can we create successful book clubs in our classrooms? The truth is, there isn't one exact formula. All book clubs are different; they can find their groove and succeed, and they can experience road bumps. Success begins with the preparation we'll need to do to start book clubs and get students excited about reading. Such preparation involves weighing our options, making purposeful decisions that best suit our students' needs, and customizing book clubs that are just right for our classroom.

Too often the logistics of setting up book clubs can feel overwhelming and complex. Many questions can bog us down and stop us in our tracks if we let them. When we begin to organize and launch book clubs, we wonder:

- Which books should I use?
- Where will I get the books? Can I use texts other than books?

- What if I haven't read all of the books?

- How will I group my students?

With so many questions and options, planning for book clubs can feel overwhelming. We've also felt anxious that we have too few books and that the groupings for the clubs aren't quite right. Over the years, we've experienced all of these issues; however, the benefits of the clubs far outweigh the occasional hurdles. And most importantly, everything can be adjusted and remedied.

Types of Book Clubs

Jayden was one of Sonja's fifth-grade students, and he loved to read non-fiction and graphic novels. During independent reading time, Jayden could be found reading a Guinness World Records book, the Amulet graphic novel series by Kazu Kibuishi, and Ripley's Believe It or Not books. When it came time for book clubs, Jayden expressed dismay. "Another historical fiction book? Why can't we read more interesting books in our clubs?" Sonja shared Jayden's response with Dana. And this experience became a turning point in our teaching. Why couldn't our students read books other than fiction? Why couldn't we have graphic novel book clubs and nonfiction book clubs? We had to adjust our mindset and recognize that there can be many different types of books clubs.

Too often, teachers only envision book clubs where students all read the same text and it's typically fiction. The truth is that book clubs can look many different ways—they don't have to be based around the same text; they don't have to be based around the same genre.

We invite you to broaden your idea of what a book club can be. In the same way that our understanding of a text goes beyond the traditional printed form to include photographs, advertisements, maps, digital images, and videos, so too must our understanding of book clubs expand. There can be various types of book clubs, even ones where participants aren't necessarily reading a book. In this digital age, it is an exciting time to reimagine how we can use a variety of texts within the book club model. And even as *what* and *how* students read continues to evolve, the term *book club* is a universal constant that represents reading in a way that speaks to children: a social experience that is fun and joyful.

When building the clubs, keep students' interests in mind, rather than just their reading level. Tamara, a fourth grader, says, "I like choosing my own book for book club because I like finding a book that calls to me and deciding if I like that genre or not." Jacob, a third-grade student, adds, "I like choosing my own book because then I don't get stuck with the worst book ever!" We smile when we hear Tamara's and Jacob's thoughts about choosing their own books. We couldn't have said it better—no one wants to have the "worst book ever." We all want to read books that "call to us." It is important for us to keep our students' interests in the forefront of our minds when we are creating book clubs. It will increase student buy-in and build excitement for reading.

When we are thinking about the many types of book clubs we can have in our classrooms, we want to caution against forming clubs based solely on reading levels. Our students can *always* sense if they're being grouped by ability, and this can cause anxiety and disappointment. As Fountas and Pinnell (2018) warn, "Labeling children by their level is detrimental to their self-esteem, their engagement, and ultimately their progress. The truth is that children can read books on a wide variety of levels . . . across the day." We have found this to be true in our book clubs. We have seen many students tackle challenging texts and find success. Fifth- and sixth-grade special education teacher Cathy Gigantino notes that "student choice and interest makes for successful book clubs. It allows for differentiation among students of varying reading levels. When students are working in book clubs, it is a great opportunity to support students in developing questions that allow for deeper understanding and great conversation. This is helpful for the students I work with because they have an opportunity to mix in with other students with the same interests." Student interest is the key to success, so students must have a say in which books they read. Therefore, part of organizing and setting up for book clubs includes helping students self-select books that will work for them no matter which type of book club they join.

GENRE-BASED BOOK CLUBS

Genre-based book clubs are the most common, but you'll have to choose from several options.

1) Each club reads the same genre, such as historical fiction, fantasy, or mystery. For example, if you want to have historical fiction book clubs, each club can read about a specific time period such as the Vietnam War, the Civil Rights Movement, or the Great Depression. Genre-based book clubs allow you to coach and teach minilessons that target skills based in that particular genre. If you choose this model, you will need multiple copies of each book so all members in the club have a copy to read.

2) Each club reads a different genre. Although one club is reading historical fiction, another might be reading realistic fiction, and yet another might be reading science fiction. This is a good option when students request a specific genre. It can also lessen the challenge for teachers to obtain multiple copies of books in just one particular genre.

3) If you've tried genre-based book clubs before, and you're looking for a way to shake them up a bit, you might want to try having each student in the club read a different book. For example, if a club is studying historical fiction and the Great Depression era, one student could be reading *Bud, Not Buddy* by Christopher Paul Curtis while another student reads *Esperanza Rising* by Pam Muñoz Ryan. This makes it possible for students to discuss a common time period and study it from different perspectives. Students may talk about what they are noticing in their book and then across the books in their group. They'll find similarities and differences, points of intersection and overlapping themes. This particular option is the most helpful if you don't have multiple copies of the same book. This also gives students more choice with book selection.

GOALS-BASED BOOK CLUBS

When teachers organize book clubs around reading goals identified by their students, it leads to greater flexibility. Student goals may include increasing volume of reading and pacing, trying new and unfamiliar genres, improving fluency when reading aloud, and so on. For instance, several students may recognize that finishing a book is challenging for them, and their book club's goal is to journey through a text from beginning to end together. It is difficult for them to read more than a few pages at a time, and a book drags along for weeks and months. These students can become a book club whose focus is primarily on reading and finishing as many books as they can within a designated time frame. One of Dana's fifth-grade book clubs wanted to complete two books during the book club unit: *President of the Whole Fifth Grade* by Sherri Winston and *El Deafo* by Cece Bell. The club members cheered each other on as they read, and by the end of book clubs, they had finished both books. For many of the students in the club, it was the first time they completed an entire book that was not assigned by a teacher. In a goals-based book club, students can discover and discuss strategies that help them to commit to a book, read with stamina, and enjoy the sweet feeling of success as their collective stack of books grows. We've seen many older students, in particular, enjoy the challenge of setting reading goals together as a book club. They enjoy the feeling of choosing what they want to read and supporting each other to meet their goals.

IDENTITY-BASED BOOK CLUBS

Recently, there has been an emergence of book clubs that allow students to have safe, candid conversations about their identities. In Figure 2.1, you can see three members of a girls-only book club reading and discussing

Figure 2.1 Three Girls in a Book Club

Restart by Gordon Korman. In these clubs, reading and discussing texts can expand the boundaries of society-imposed gender norms and provide a space for girls to explore other ways of being. Less frequently explored, perhaps, are boys-only book clubs. These spaces give boys the opportunity to do the type of reading that truly interests them. For example, at Truesdale Education Campus in Washington, DC, educators are interrupting the narrative about African American boys and reading with a boys-only book club. For boys of color, being able to encounter characters who look like them and to read stories that are reflective of their lives has helped them to become ravenous readers, according to Truesdale. Identity-based book clubs can be created by students based on gender, race, religion, and sexual orientation. They are opportunities to affirm students' identities in spaces where they feel valued, included, and empowered.

THEME- AND TOPIC-BASED BOOK CLUBS

Our students enter our classrooms with specific interests they hope will be validated and nurtured. In theme-based and topic-based book clubs, students can explore their passions with like-minded peers. Sean, a sixth grader, was able to nurture his love of superheroes and the theme of good versus evil in a comic book club. Sean and his peers explored this theme as they read the Avengers and the Fantastic Four comic books. Whatever the topic or theme (environmental concerns, social justice issues, STEM— science, technology, engineering, and mathematics), students are motivated and engaged when reading texts about topics that are important to them. In Figure 2.2 you will find a sample of themes and topics students may want to explore in their book club.

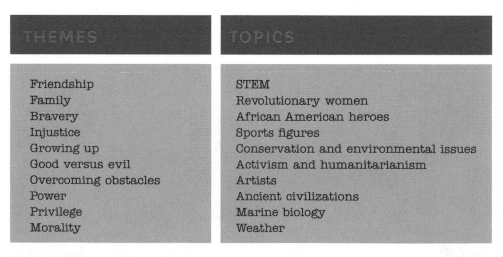

THEMES	TOPICS
Friendship	STEM
Family	Revolutionary women
Bravery	African American heroes
Injustice	Sports figures
Growing up	Conservation and environmental issues
Good versus evil	Activism and humanitarianism
Overcoming obstacles	Artists
Power	Ancient civilizations
Privilege	Marine biology
Morality	Weather

Figure 2.2 Sample Themes and Topics

SERIES- AND AUTHOR-BASED BOOK CLUBS

Series- and author-based book clubs are great opportunities for teachers to utilize different types of books in their classrooms and for students to linger with series and authors they love. Lucy Calkins and the Teachers College Reading and Writing Project (TCRWP) recommend series-based book clubs for young readers, because students can read stacks of books over the course of a couple of weeks. In addition, in series book clubs, students become experts about characters. Likewise, author-based book clubs provide opportunities for students to appreciate the range and craft of specific writers. Author-based studies can be done with picture books, novels, or a blend of both.

ONLINE BOOK CLUBS

Several types of book clubs can thrive in and outside our classrooms. Online book clubs in particular provide access for students who have distinct reading passions. Consider students like Mark, who in sixth grade was a nonfiction buff. He took a particular interest in politics and history. For Mark and a few of his peers, an online book club made the most sense. It enabled them to nurture their reading interests by accessing websites such as Newsela.com, TimeforKids.com, and even NYTimes.com. Each of these websites makes it possible for students to search for specific topics such as, in the case of Mark's book club, the Syrian civil war, the removal of Confederate monuments, and the Flint, Michigan, water crisis. And for students like fourth-grader Tiana and her peers, reading about science was their passion. With an online subscription to *Muse* magazine, Tiana's book club was able to read about a variety of science topics and connect with other students globally who have similar interests using the website's ePals component (with their teacher's guidance). Additionally, online book clubs allowed Joaquin and his peers to develop their love of short stories. Cricketmagkids.com, Freechildrenstories.com, and Stonesoup.com became their go-to websites to read short stories written by kids like them from around the country. One member of this book club was so inspired by the short stories he read, he wrote one himself and submitted it to *Stone Soup* magazine, and it was chosen for publication!

Today's book clubs recognize the ways students engage with information as well as how they read. Online book clubs provide students with options for accessing and expressing information as well as connecting and collaborating with peers. In a technology-rich landscape, educators can tap into the ways students, particularly teens, connect with their peers by encouraging the use of blogs and other platforms that can be used to meet and discuss texts. This is a great option for older students in classes with shorter literacy blocks than their younger peers. For example, students might utilize Google Classroom or other digital platforms to have online discussions with their peers. Teachers can observe students' insights and make coaching decisions that will support their learning.

Getting the Books

Book Lists, p. 33

One of the biggest hurdles educators face is lack of books. Club groupings can be as small (two or three students) or as large (five or six students) as you need. For this reason, it may be possible for you to secure a few copies of the same book from your classroom, the school library, and possibly another classroom in your building. If clubs are larger, you may need to find alternate ways of securing the books:

- Pool resources with colleagues across your building and create a bookroom.

- Visit used book fairs/drives not only in your school district but in neighboring schools.

- Check for book sales at public libraries in your area.

- Consider including book titles on a supply list or wish list that is sent home to families over the summer or provided during Back to School Night.

Over Time

- Apply for a Parent Teacher Student Association grant to grow your classroom library, specifically to obtain multiple copies of books for book clubs.

- Use your Scholastic book points to purchase multiple sets of books.

It's All About the Books: How to Create Bookrooms and Classroom Libraries by Tammy Mulligan and Clare Landrigan (2018) is an invaluable resource for teachers who are looking for ways to acquire books and pool their resources.

One way to breathe new life into book clubs is to commit to acquiring new books. At times, we can become attached to the titles of books we love and are emotionally invested in our students loving them. The books we loved when we were our students' age may not be those they love now. In fact, it is possible that our students disconnect from reading because of the challenge of seeing themselves in some of the stories they are invited to read, stories where their lives and circumstances are virtually invisible. Poet Adrienne Rich said, "When someone with the authority of a teacher describes the world and you are not in it, there is a moment of psychic disequilibrium, as if you looked into a mirror and saw nothing" (1994, 199). Adrienne Rich reminds us that as teachers we hold a powerful platform. And from this platform we have the power to include, affirm, and celebrate by making conscious decisions about the books we make available in our classrooms.

When we choose books for book clubs, we provide opportunities for students to see themselves and to learn about the lives of others. Jacqueline Woodson, one of our author heroes, shares that it is "important that if your school system is not racially or economically or diverse in terms of gender, that the books still reflect that because the kids need to meet people unlike themselves and find a place in those people and in the story" (Reading Rockets 2014). We Need Diverse Books (https://diversebooks.org) is an essential resource for all educators to utilize to learn about the books that are available about characters and by authors from diverse backgrounds. This needs to be a priority for all teachers. Seeing themselves reflected in texts and learning about others different from themselves allow our students to grow into change makers and become active participants in a democratic society.

Additionally, we want to make sure that all of our students have opportunities to have a positive reading experience in book clubs. When selecting books particularly for English language learner students, Jenice Mateo-Toledo, an English language learner educator for grades 6–11, says, "When running book clubs, one of the biggest challenges I've faced is selecting books that contain content that is appropriate for older readers but is written within lower Lexile levels. Another challenge I've experienced is discovering books with authentic voice, devoid of stereotypes, that focus on the immigrant experience in respectful and sensitive ways." We've relied on Jenice's

Figure 2.3 Girls' Book Club on the Carpet

expertise in this area when selecting books that speak to our students' wide range of needs and experiences. (See Figure 2.3 for a girls' book club meeting on the carpet.)

Book Clubs Checklist

Before launching book clubs, it is vital to prepare. This process can be broken down into three key questions: Where will I get enough copies of books? How do I group my students? What type of book clubs do I want to offer? Your answers to these questions will help guide you through the initial steps of planning your clubs. Figure 2.4 shows how Dana used the Book Clubs Checklist to help plan her author-based book clubs. We recommend that you use the Book Clubs Checklist in Figure 2.5, available in the Online Resources, to help you get started.

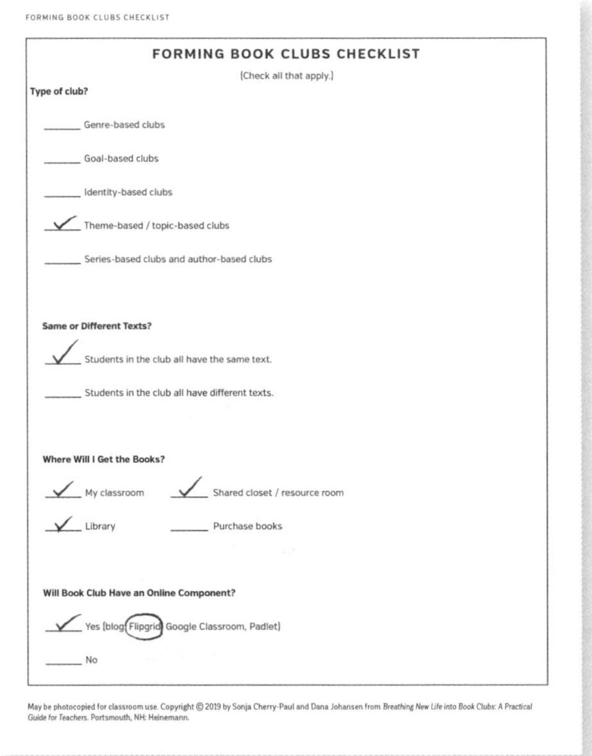

FORMING BOOK CLUBS CHECKLIST

FORMING BOOK CLUBS CHECKLIST

[Check all that apply.]

Type of club?

_____ Genre-based clubs

_____ Goal-based clubs

_____ Identity-based clubs

✓ Theme-based / topic-based clubs

_____ Series-based clubs and author-based clubs

Same or Different Texts?

✓ Students in the club all have the same text.

_____ Students in the club all have different texts.

Where Will I Get the Books?

✓ My classroom   ✓ Shared closet / resource room

✓ Library   _____ Purchase books

Will Book Club Have an Online Component?

✓ Yes [blog, (Flipgrid,) Google Classroom, Padlet]

_____ No

May be photocopied for classroom use. Copyright © 2019 by Sonja Cherry-Paul and Dana Johansen from *Breathing New Life into Book Clubs: A Practical Guide for Teachers*. Portsmouth, NH: Heinemann.

Figure 2.4 (left)
Completed Book Clubs Checklist

Figure 2.5 (below)
Forming Book Clubs Checklist

FORMING BOOK CLUBS CHECKLIST

FORMING BOOK CLUBS CHECKLIST

[Check all that apply.]

Type of club?

_____ Genre-based clubs

_____ Goal-based clubs

_____ Identity-based clubs

_____ Theme-based / topic-based clubs

_____ Series-based clubs and author-based clubs

Same or Different Texts?

_____ Students in the club all have the same text.

_____ Students in the club all have different texts.

Where Will I Get the Books?

_____ My classroom   _____ Shared closet / resource room

_____ Library   _____ Purchase books

Will Book Club Have an Online Component?

_____ Yes [blog, Flipgrid, Google Classroom, Padlet]

_____ No

May be photocopied for classroom use. Copyright © 2019 by Sonja Cherry-Paul and Dana Johansen from *Breathing New Life into Book Clubs: A Practical Guide for Teachers*. Portsmouth, NH: Heinemann.

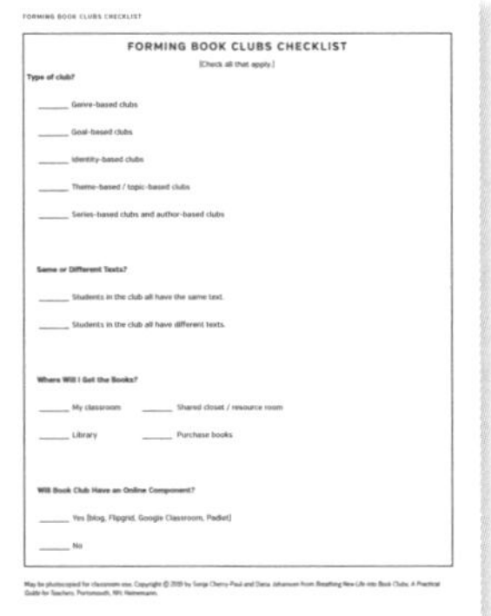

Drumming Up Excitement for Book Clubs

You can drum up excitement for book clubs by making changes to the physical space of your classroom and advertising the books that students can choose from. Picture a Monday morning and your students are walking into the classroom. They greet you with warm, tired Monday morning smiles. However, this Monday is different. Your students' eyes brighten and widen as they look around the room and notice some changes to the physical space of the classroom. They see stacks of books on a bookshelf with a large sign that says, "Coming Soon! Book Clubs!" They also see a new bulletin board that says "Room 7 Book Clubs," and they notice a special place on the board for each club to display its name and banner. As your students look around the classroom, their excitement grows. They eagerly begin asking questions, such as "What are book clubs?" and "Do we get to read all those books?" and "When do the clubs start?" This is the enthusiastic kickoff we envision for book clubs.

We want our students to be on the edge of their seats in anticipation for the start of book clubs. Gathering and displaying the books over a brief period of time before the clubs begin will get students itching to read. In addition, many educators use book talks and book trailers to introduce students to book club titles. Some teachers whet students' appetites for reading by presenting authors' biographies or tweeting with the author. When we present book clubs as special and exciting, our students treasure the time they have to read and engage with their peers. To pique your students' interest in book clubs, you can change aspects of the physical classroom environment. We recommend creating book displays, bulletin boards, cozy book club nooks, and class messages.

CREATIVE BOOK DISPLAYS

Line the books on a shelf and create a sign such as "Get Excited for Book Clubs!" Another possibility is to use a "red carpet" and have the books lined up. The sign might say, "Today's Stars Are . . ." Or perhaps you want to cause a bit of a book frenzy and arrange your books on a shelf and tape them off like the display on page 16. You can create a sign saying "Do Not Touch: Book Clubs Coming Soon!" This makes the books irresistible, since students are drawn to off-limit books like moths to a flame!

BULLETIN BOARDS

You can use the board to announce the titles of the book club books and display students' upcoming work such as club banners, flags, and writing.

CLASSROOM DOORS AND CLUBHOUSES

We love decorating our classroom doors with book jackets, interesting quotes, and other images that spark our students' interest in book clubs. Additionally, we have built clubhouses for our students. Figure 2.6 shows an example of a clubhouse in a fifth-grade classroom. These

Figure 2.6 Clubhouse

cardboard structures are easy to build, and the best part is that they are fully collapsible. You can pull them out of the closet for book clubs and then easily tuck them back in when the clubs are over.

MORNING MESSAGES / CLASS WEBSITES

If you write your students a morning meeting message each day, this is a great place to get them excited about book clubs. In addition, if you have a class website or a newsletter, you may also want to inform your students there that book clubs are on the horizon.

Talking Up the Books

Depending on the number of books you plan to feature in book clubs, rolling out the books to your students may take a short or extended amount of time. In other words, you might roll out all the books in a day or it might take a week to roll out the books little by little. Students should have their writing utensils at the ready, so they can jot down the titles they're interested in reading.

It is possible that you will have read many, if not all, of the books featured in book clubs. But it is a common misconception that teachers need to read every book. It's simply not a reality for all teachers—including us! Some teachers worry that they cannot recommend a book that they haven't read. However, there are several options that can help us with this challenge.

BOOK TALKS

If you have read the books offered to clubs, a book talk is a great option to get students excited about reading. Book talks are short sales pitches that inspire your students to want to read the book. They include three parts: a short description of the overall plot of the book, a short excerpt or quote, and a few sentences such as "If you're a reader who likes . . ." or "If you want to learn more about . . ." Book talks pique students' interest in the books, and even if they do not choose to read that particular book during book clubs, they may choose to read it independently.

GUEST BOOK TALKS

Building a community of readers involves reading role models. Share videos of featured authors, such as Jason Reynolds (Left Bank Books 2016), who talks about the importance of reading. Inviting former students, guest teachers, or librarians to give a book talk is another fun way to show your students that there are reading role models all around them.

BOOK TRAILERS

A book trailer is just like a movie trailer. There are many book trailers online that give students a sneak peek at the book's plot and appeal. To find premade book trailers, you can search your book club titles in YouTube. Trailers for Veronica Roth's *Divergent* (harperteen 2011) and Kate DiCamillo's *Raymie Nightingale* (Candlewick Press 2016) are two fan favorites. Our students love watching book trailers prior to choosing which book they want to read in their clubs. The best part about book trailers is that if you haven't read the book yourself, a book trailer promotes the book for you. Your students can also make their own book trailers at the end of book clubs, and you can use these trailers with future students.

BOOK BLOGS

If you have a digital platform, you can create intriguing posts about the books. For example, if you use Padlet with your class, you might post images of the books available for book clubs, along with a short description. If you have a class website, you may want to post images and descriptions online, so your students can peruse each title and get a sense of which books they might want to read.

FREE EXPLORATION

One of our favorite ways to help students decide which books they may want to read is to provide time for free exploration with the books. We place a stack of the books in the center of the desk clusters and invite students to hold each book in their hands, examine the cover, read the back or book flap, and try the first page (see Figure 2.7).

Figure 2.7 Book Shopping

Even if you have book talked all the books, it is still important for your students to examine the books and see if they are a good fit. This is also a great option if you haven't read all the books yourself.

Helping Students Choose Their Book

The hallmark of a successful book club is student buy-in. As seventh-grader Lily says, "I like picking my own books because I don't always like the books we read if the teacher picks them. This way we have our own say." We've seen clubs fail over the years because the teacher chose the books that students read in their clubs. Students had no choice, and as a result, their engagement was low. Without choice, you will hear choruses of "I don't want to read this book." "I've already read this book." "I want to read a different book." Also, when students aren't given a choice, they will think that book clubs are grouped by reading level. This does not set the right tone at the beginning of book clubs. Erica Williams, sixth- to eighth-grade English teacher, says, "I always try to assign students their first or second choice of text, and sometimes this means grouping together students I know won't necessarily gel. It then becomes a decision of whether or not to give the students the benefit of the doubt and see how they end up working together (Who knows? Maybe they'll surprise me!), or assign them a book that was low on their list of choices." When students get their "first- or second-choice" book, it instills a sense of ownership and joy for reading.

It is important to teach your students *how* to choose books that are a good fit for them. If you are working with younger students, you may be encouraging them to use the popular Five Finger strategy for finding "just-right" books. In this strategy, students turn to a random page in the text and count how many words are unfamiliar to them. If they reach five, they are encouraged to choose a different book that may be easier for them to read independently. However, we encourage you to prioritize a child's interest and choice over ease in readability. The discussions in book clubs act as a great scaffold for students who are encountering challenges reading the book independently. If the child's interest in the book is strong, he or she will persevere and enjoy the conversations with fellow book club members. We've seen many students purposefully take on the challenge of reading a more complex text in a book club because the stakes are low. It's a great opportunity for students to take risks.

Older students tend to choose books based on their peers' recommendations and their gut reactions to the cover, first few pages, and genre. We've found that older students need time to hold the books and listen to their peers' recommendations. This makes sense, as adults go through a similar process. Many teachers get book recommendations from lunchroom table discussions, the *New York Times* bestseller list, Twitter chats, and online book clubs.

It can be difficult to always honor your students' top choices. Jeff Schwartz, ninth- to twelfth-grade English teacher, noted, "I was surprised by how challenging it would be to honor students' top choices. I wanted them to read in groups of three to four, but this meant balancing choices and, in some cases, their abilities based on working with them this year.

Once we established groups, I found it really helpful to give them clear expectations but also to empower them to create their own schedule. They finished books faster—and enjoyed them as much as or more—than all-class books." Like Jeff, we have found that although the groups may have different numbers of students, choice is most important. Ultimately, you can decide how much choice you want to give your students. There are a range of options.

PICK 3

Display all the book club books on a counter or bookshelf. Next, students write down the titles of three books they'd like to read. These titles go on their "Pick 3" list. Be sure to explain to students that they are not ranking their choices from favorite to least favorite. Instead, they are simply listing three books they'd be open to reading. This gives teachers greater flexibility in creating the groupings. Next, the teacher can create the book clubs based on the students' preferences. This strategy can be modified to a "Pick 5" list, and so on. This strategy provides the perfect balance of choice. Students have a say about their book, and teachers have a say about the club groupings.

RANK ORDER THE BOOKS

Students are given a selection of 3–5 book titles that they can rank order based on their preference. This strategy works best with older students in upper middle school grades and high school. Figure 2.8 shows Devon's titles in order of preference. The teacher can make sure that students are engaged in their reading because they ranked the book high on their list. We've seen great success using this approach with both older students and reluctant readers.

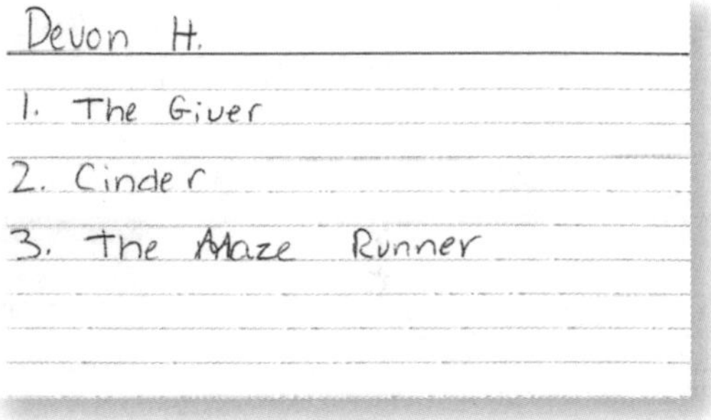

Devon H.

1. The Giver
2. Cinder
3. The Maze Runner

Figure 2.8 Devon's Ranked List

THE CHOICE IS YOURS!

This approach allows students to pick a book they're interested in reading, and then the club is based around what the students choose. With this option, students do not need to make a list. They simply walk up to the display of books and choose what they'd like to read. Although students enjoy having so much choice, keep in mind that it is important to think about groupings and managing the social dynamics.

Creating the Club Groups

Now that your students have chosen the books they'd like to read, it is time to make the groups. We like to consider our students' book requests and the social dynamics of the class. As teachers, we have a keen sense for grouping students who will work well together. We've discovered that choice and ownership are what matter most when forming successful book club groups.

Sometimes, even the best-laid plans are not fruitful. If, at any point, you find that a book club is not successful, we offer strategies in Chapter 3 for how to help reenergize the group or help students abandon the book to try something else. Maureen Corbo, sixth-grade English teacher and leader of her school's Mock Newbery Club, reflected on her experiences with creating book club groups. She said, "When I first started doing book clubs, I found grouping the students to be very stressful. I hated when students said that they didn't like the book and wanted to switch. Now those types of issues don't bother me as much—I just want to get things going and keep 'em moving!" We've also found that the best way to stay organized while making the book club groups is to use a template like the one in Figure 2.9. Here Sonja has organized her students into historical fiction book clubs based on time periods. A blank form, shown in Figure 2.10, can be found in the Online Resources.

Figure 2.9 (left)
Completed Clubs
Diagrams Template

Figure 2.10 (below)
Clubs Diagrams

Figure 2.9 content:

CLUBS DIAGRAMS

CLUBS DIAGRAMS

CLUB 1	CLUB 2	CLUB 3
Type of Club: Historical Fiction (Great Depression)	Type of Club: Historical Fiction (Civil Rights Movement)	Type of Club: Historical Fiction (Vietnam War)
Book: Bud, Not Buddy by Christopher Paul Curtis	Book: One Crazy Summer by Rita Williams-Garcia	Book: Shooting the Moon by Frances O'Roark Dowell
Club Members: Owen Jackie Christopher Lena	Club Members: Dahlia Terry Graham Spencer	Club Members: Julia Jacob Darren Ava

CLUB 4	CLUB 5	CLUB 6
Type of Club: Historical Fiction (WWII)	Type of Club: Historical Fiction (WWII)	Type of Club:
Book: The War that Saved My Life by Kimberly Brubaker Bradley	Book: Sylvia + Aki by Winifred Conklin	Book:
Club Members: Paul Devin Asia Jackson Maria	Club Members: Joaquin Beth Ashley Charlie	Club Members:

It is important to note that not every student will want to be in a book club. Listen to the needs of your students. Forcing students to take part in a book club runs the risk of increasing anxiety and producing a negative view of reading. In cases such as these, let's instead honor our students' wishes and support their development as readers through independent reading experiences or partnerships in lieu of book clubs. Students can also access audiobooks if they'd like, and create reading and written response plans like students in book clubs. Don't lose sight of the most important goal: cultivating a love of reading!

Breathing New Life into Organizing Book Clubs

Disney's Buzz Lightyear says, "To infinity, and beyond!" We think of these words every time we have a chance to refresh and breathe new life into the curricula. There is unlimited potential for the ways we can reimagine our book clubs. Everything from the forming of clubs, to rethinking the book options, to getting our students pumped for reading, to providing different opportunities for our students to have ownership over the books they *really* want to read.

We invite you to take a few minutes, and pause here to reflect on the possibilities. After reading this chapter, what is still percolating for you? What might you try differently the next time you have book clubs?

Chapter Two Resources at a Glance

IDEAS	SPECIFICS	RESOURCES
Think flexibly! Consider different types of book clubs, which lead to greater possibilities and increased reading engagement for students.	**Which type of book club meets the needs of my students?** Try a new type of book club: • Genre-based • Goal-based • Identity-based • Theme- or topic-based • Series-based • Online	**Forming Book Clubs Checklist** p. 24
Plan and prepare! Customize book clubs that are just right for your students and your classrooms.	**Which books should I make available, and where will I get them?** Use a variety of ways to acquire books: • Borrow from colleagues • Visit book fairs and book sales at libraries • Add book titles to supply/wish lists • Apply for PTA grant	**Book club book lists:** **Grade 3 Book Club Bins** p. 34 **Grade 4 Book Club Bins** p. 36 **Grade 5 Book Club Bins** p. 38 **Grade 6 Book Club Bins** p. 40 **Grade 7 Book Club Bins** p. 42 **Grade 8 Book Club Bins** p. 44
Drum up excitement! Whet students' appetites with activities that put them on the edge of their seats in anticipation for the start of book clubs.	**How do I set the tone for book clubs so students treasure this time to read and engage with their peers?** Present book clubs as special and exciting: • Creative book displays • Morning messages/class websites • Book talks • Book blogs	**Clubhouses** p. 25 **Book Trailers** p. 27 *Divergent* **by Veronica Roth:** https://youtu.be/tu5Erw-posg *Raymie Nightingale* **by Kate DiCamillo:** https://youtube /65ByjC7v_EE **Guest Book Talks** p. 26 *Harbor Me* **by Jacqueline Woodson:** https://www .youtube.com/watch?v =FjKqwqpBgGM **Jason Reynolds, "Why It's Important for Kids to Read":** https://youtu.be/ATeoup5a-XU
Help students choose books! Instill a sense of ownership and joy for reading in book clubs.	**How do I group students and teach them to choose books that are a good fit?** Provide choice using a range of options: • Pick 3 • Rank order • The choice is yours! • Club groupings	**Book Clubs Diagram** p. 30

Grade 3 Book Club Bins

Realistic Fiction

A Boy Called Bat by Elana K. Arnold

Alvin Ho: Allergic to Girls, School, and Other Things by Lenore Look

Brand New School, Brave New Ruby by Derrick Barnes

Freckle Juice by Judy Blume

Honey by Sarah Weeks

How to Eat Fried Worms by Thomas Rockwell

Jupiter Storm by Marti Dumas

The Lemonade War by Jacqueline Davies

Mystery Fiction Series

A to Z Mysteries series by Ron Roy

Boxcar Children series by Gertrude Chandler Warner

Clubhouse Mysteries series by Sharon Draper

Encyclopedia Brown series by Donald J. Sobol

Key Hunters series by Eric Luper

Sherlock Academy series by F. C. Shaw

The Great Shelby Holmes series by Elizabeth Eulberg

Historical Fiction Series

Blast to the Past series by Stacia Deutsch and Rhody Cohon

Dear America series

I Survived series by Lauren Tarshis

Magic Tree House series by Mary Pope Osborne

My America series by assorted authors

Ranger in Time series by Kate Messner

Fantasy Fiction

Dragon Slayers Academy series by Kate McMullan

James and the Giant Peach by Roald Dahl

Nadia Knox and the Eye of Zinnia by Jessica McDougle

Sideways Stories from Wayside School by Louis Sachar

The Chocolate Touch by Patrick Skene Catling

The Doll People by Ann Martin and Laura Godwin

The Mouse and the Motorcycle by Beverly Cleary

The Tail of Emily Windsnap by Liz Kessler

Graphic Novels

Babymouse series by Jennifer L. Holm and Matthew Holm

Bake Sale by Sara Varon

Dragonbreath series by Ursula Vernon

Lunch Lady series by Jarrett J. Krosoczka

Magic Pickle series by Scott Morse

Narwhal: Unicorn of the Sea by Ben Clanton

Secret Coders series by Gene Luen Yang

Squish: Super Amoeba by Jennifer L. Holm and Matthew Holm

Patricia Polacco Author Study

Chicken Sunday

Holes in the Sky

Mr. Lincoln's Way

Pink and Say

Thank You, Mr. Falker

The Junkyard Wonders

The Keeping Quilt

The Lemonade Club

Animal Series

Dog Whisperer series by Nicholas
    Edwards
Hero series by Jennifer Li Shotz
Pet Hotel series by Kate Finch
Shelter Pet Squad series by Cynthia
    Lord
The Puppy Place series by Ellen
    Miles
Vet Volunteers series by Laurie
    Halse Anderson

Friendship

Charlotte's Web by E. B. White
Frindle by Andrew Clements
The Hundred Dresses by Eleanor
    Estes
The Magnificent Mya Tibbs by
    Crystal Allen
The One and Only Ivan by Katherine
    Applegate
The Wild Robot by Peter Brown
The Year of the Three Sisters by
    Andrea Cheng
Where the Mountain Meets the Moon
    by Grace Lin

Nonfiction Series

101 History Facts series by IP Factly
Heroes of History series by the
    editors of *Time*
If You Lived . . . series by assorted
    authors
Who Was? series by assorted
    authors
You Wouldn't Want to . . . series by
    assorted authors

Grade 4 Book Club Bins

Realistic Fiction

Cheese by Sarah Weeks
Gaby, Lost and Found by Angela Cervantes
Rules by Cynthia Lord
Tales of a Fourth Grade Nothing by Judy Blume
The Sweetest Sound by Sherri Winston
The Thing About Georgie by Lisa Graff
The Year of the Dog by Grace Lin
Two Naomis by Olugbemisola Rhuday-Perkovich and Audrey Vernick

Mystery Fiction

Capture the Flag by Kate Messner
Eddie Red Undercover series by Marcia Wells
Pie by Sarah Weeks
Sammy Keyes series by Wendelin Van Draanen
Swindle by Gordon Korman
The Doublecross by Jackson Pearce
The Genius Files series by Dan Gutman
The Secret series by Pseudonymous Bosch

Historical Fiction

Dash by Kirby Larson
Full of Beans by Jennifer L. Holm
Glory Be by Augusta Scattergood
Number the Stars by Lois Lowry
Paper Wishes by Lois Sepahban
Rickshaw Girl by Mitali Perkins
Snow Treasure by Marie McSwigan
Sugar by Jewell Parker Rhodes

Fantasy Fiction

11 Birthdays by Wendy Mass
13 Treasures by Michelle Harrison
Harry Potter series by J. K. Rowling
Joshua Dread by Lee Bacon
The Lion, the Witch, and the Wardrobe by C. S. Lewis
The Pepins and Their Problems by Polly Horvath
The School for Good and Evil by Soman Chainani
The Uncommoners by Jennifer Bell

Graphic Novels

Dog Man by Dav Pilkey
El Deafo by Cece Bell
Mighty Jack by Ben Hatke
Redwall: The Graphic Novel by Brian Jacques
Sisters by Raina Telgemeier
Smile by Raina Telgemeier
The Nameless City by Faith Erin Hicks
Zita the Spacegirl by Ben Hatke

Strong Female Protagonists

A Handful of Stars by Cynthia Lord
All Four Stars by Tara Dairman
Audacity Jones to the Rescue by Kirby Larson
Our Only May Amelia by Jennifer L. Holm
President of the Whole Fifth Grade by Sherri Winston
The Key to Extraordinary by Natalie Lloyd
The Year of the Rat by Grace Lin
When the Sea Turned to Silver by Grace Lin

Kate DiCamillo Author Study

Because of Winn-Dixie
Flora and Ulysses
The Magician's Elephant
*The Miraculous Journey of Edward
   Tulane*
The Tale of Despereaux
The Tiger Rising

Animal Series

A Dog's Purpose Puppy Tales series
   by W. Bruce Cameron
Animorphs series by K. A. Applegate
Survivors by Erin Hunter
The Familiars by Adam Jay Epstein
   and Andrew Jacobson
The Menagerie by Tui T. Sutherland
   and Kari H. Sutherland
The Secret Zoo by Bryan Chick
Warriors: Into the Wild by Erin
   Hunter

Nonfiction: Marine Biology, Sharks, and Dolphins

*Discovery Channel Sharkopedia: The
   Complete Guide to Everything
   Shark* by Discovery Channel
*National Geographic Kids Everything
   Dolphins: Dolphin Facts, Photos,
   and Fun That Will Make You Flip*
   by Elizabeth Carney
*National Geographic Kids Everything
   Sharks: All the Shark Facts,
   Photos, and Fun That You Can
   Sink Your Teeth Into* by Ruth
   Musgrave
Oceans by Seymour Simon
Sharks by Seymour Simon
*Ultimate Oceanpedia: The Most
   Complete Ocean Reference Ever*
   [National Geographic Kids] by
   Christina Wilsdon

Grade 5 Book Club Bins

Realistic Fiction

Amina's Voice by Hena Khan

A Whole New Ballgame by Phil Bildner

Because of Mr. Terupt by Rob Buyea

Out of My Mind by Sharon M. Draper

Save Me a Seat by Sarah Weeks and Gita Varadarajan

The Blossoming Universe of Violet Diamond by Brenda Woods

The Turtle of Oman by Naomi Shihab Nye

Wonder by R. J. Palacio

Mystery Fiction

Chasing Vermeer by Blue Balliett

Fuzzy Mud by Louis Sachar

Greenglass House by Kate Milford

Masterminds by Gordon Korman

Mr. Lemoncello's Library by Chris Grabenstein

Quicksand Pond by Janet Taylor Lisle

Saving Kabul Corner by N. H. Senzai

Space Case by Stuart Gibbs

The Ghosts of Tupelo Landing by Sheila Turnage

Historical Fiction

Esperanza Rising by Pam Muñoz Ryan

Inside Out and Back Again by Thanhha Lai

Red Berries, White Clouds, Blue Sky by Sandra Dallas

Stella by Starlight by Sharon M. Draper

Sylvia & Aki by Winifred Conkling

The Liberation of Gabriel King by K. L. Going

The War That Saved My Life by Kimberly Brubaker Bradley

The Watsons Go to Birmingham—1963 by Christopher Paul Curtis

Fantasy Fiction

All the Answers by Kate Messner

Aru Shah and the End of Time by Roshani Chokshi

A Tale Dark and Grimm by Adam Gidwitz

Powerless by Matthew Cody

Savvy by Ingrid Law

The Gauntlet by Karuna Riazi

The Land of Stories by Chris Colfer

The Secret Spiral by Gillian Neimark

The Sisters Grimm series by Michael Buckley

Wings of Fire series by Tui T. Sutherland

Graphic Novels

Amulet series by Kazu Kibuishi

Bone series by Jeff Smith

Cleopatra in Space series by Mike Maihack

Drowned City by Don Brown

Mighty Jack by Ben Hatke

Page by Paige by Laura Lee Gulledge

Robot Dreams by Sara Varon

Roller Girl by Victoria Jamieson

Sharon Creech Author Study

Bloomability

Chasing Redbird

Granny Torrelli Makes Soup

Hate That Cat

Love That Dog

Moo

The Great Unexpected

Walk Two Moons

Mythology Series

Gods of Manhattan series by Scott Mebus

Mark of the Thief series by Jennifer A. Nielsen

Pandora series by Carolyn Hennesy

Pegasus series by Kate O'Hearn

Percy Jackson series by Rick Riordan

Seven Wonders series by Peter Lerangis

The Cronus Chronicles series by Anne Ursu

The Kane Chronicles series by Rick Riordan

Overcoming Obstacles

Crash by Jerry Spinelli

Fish in a Tree by Lynda Mullaly Hunt

Holes by Louis Sachar

Lost in the Sun by Lisa Graff

Maniac Magee by Jerry Spinelli

Restart by Gordon Korman

The Key That Swallowed Joey Pigza by Jack Gantos

You Go First by Erin Entrada Kelly

Nonfiction: Forensics and History's Mysteries

Bones Never Lie: How Forensics Helps Solve History's Mysteries by Elizabeth MacLeod

Case Closed? Nine Mysteries Unlocked by Modern Science by Susan Hughes

CSI Expert! Forensic Science for Kids by Karen Schulz

Don't Read This Book Before Bed: Thrills, Chills, and Hauntingly True Stories by Anna Claybourne

Haunted Histories: Creepy Castles, Dark Dungeons, and Powerful Palaces by J. H. Everett

History's Mysteries: Curious Clues, Cold Cases, and Puzzles from the Past (National Geographic Kids) by Kitson Jazynka

Unsolved! Mysterious Places (Time for Kids Nonfiction Readers) by Teacher Created Materials

Grade 6 Book Club Bins

Realistic Fiction

Amal Unbound by Aisha Saeed
Becoming Naomi León by Pam
　Muñoz Ryan
Harbor Me by Jacqueline Woodson
Hello, Universe by Erin Entrada Kelly
Just Under the Clouds by Melissa
　Sarno
Merci Suárez Changes Gears by Meg
　Medina
Nine, Ten: A September 11 Story by
　Nora Raleigh Baskin
Schooled by Gordon Korman
The Great Wall of Lucy Wu by Wendy
　Wan-Long Shang
The Whole Story of Half a Girl by
　Veera Hiranandani

Suspense

A Properly Unhaunted Place by
　William Alexander
Doll Bones by Holly Black
Horizon by Scott Westerfeld
Spy School by Stuart Gibbs
The Calder Game by Blue Balliett
The Harlem Charade by Natasha
　Tarpley
The Parker Inheritance by Varian
　Johnson
The Van Gogh Deception by Deron
　Hicks
Three Times Lucky by Sheila Turnage
When You Reach Me by Rebecca
　Stead

Historical Fiction

Bud, Not Buddy by Christopher Paul
　Curtis
Counting on Grace by Elizabeth
　Winthrop
One Crazy Summer by Rita Williams-
　Garcia
Paperboy by Vince Vawter
Shooting the Moon by Frances
　O'Roark Dowell
Turtle in Paradise by Jennifer Holm
Wolf Hollow by Lauren Wolk

Fantasy Fiction

Fablehaven by Brandon Mull
Keeper of the Lost Cities by Shannon
　Messenger
*Nevermoor: The Trials of Morrigan
　Crow* by Jessica Townsend
*The Charmed Children of Rookskill
　Castle* by Janet Fox
The Girl Who Drank the Moon by
　Kelly Barnhill
The Unwanteds by Lisa McMann
Wishtree by Katherine Applegate

Graphic Novels

All's Faire in Middle School by
　Victoria Jamieson
Awkward by Svetlana Chmakova
Brave by Svetlana Chmakova
Drama by Raina Telgemeier
Invisible Emmie by Terri Libenson
Lumberjanes series by assorted
　authors
Nightlights by Lorena Alvarez
Pashmina by Nidhi Chanani
Real Friends by Shannon Hale
The Last Kids on Earth by Max
　Brallier

Verse Novels

Brown Girl Dreaming by Jacqueline Woodson

Forget Me Not by Ellie Terry

Full Cicada Moon by Marilyn Hilton

House Arrest by K. A. Holt

Lion Island by Margarita Engle

Rebound by Kwame Alexander

Sweetgrass Basket by Marlene Carvell

The Crazy Man by Pamela Porter

Under the Mesquite by Guadalupe Garcia McCall

Starting Over: Migration/Immigration

A Long Walk to Water by Linda Sue Park

Escape from Aleppo by N. H. Senzai

Front Desk by Kelly Yang

It Ain't So Awful, Falafel by Firoozeh Dumas

Refugee by Alan Gratz

Shooting Kabul by N. H. Senzai

The Circuit by Francisco Jiménez

The Red Pencil by Andrea Davis Pinkney

Carl Hiaasen Author Study/Environmentalism

Chomp

Flush

Hoot

Scat

Squirm

Nonfiction: Animals, Migration, Conservation

An Extraordinary Life: The Story of a Monarch Butterfly by Laurence Pringle

Beastly Brains: Exploring How Animals Think, Talk, and Feel by Nancy Castaldo

Exploding Ants: Amazing Facts About How Animals Adapt by Joanne Settel

Extreme Animals: The Toughest Creatures on Earth by Nicola Davies

Great Migrations: Whales, Wildebeests, Butterflies, Elephants, and Other Amazing Animals on the Move (National Geographic Kids) by Elizabeth Carney

Kakapo Rescue: Saving the World's Strangest Parrot by Sy Montgomery

Scaly Spotted Feathered Frilled: How Do We Know What Dinosaurs Really Looked Like? by Catherine Thimmesh

Sniffer Dogs: How Dogs (and Their Noses) Save the World by Nancy Castaldo

The Signs Animals Leave by Frank Staub

Grade 7 Book Club Bins

Realistic Fiction

Blackbird Fly by Erin Entrada Kelly
Booked by Kwame Alexander
Clayton Byrd Goes Underground by
   Rita Williams-Garcia
Ghost Boys by Jewell Parker Rhodes
Mango Delight by Fracaswell Hyman
Stef Soto Taco Queen by Jennifer
   Torres
The Crossover by Kwame Alexander
The Stars Beneath Our Feet by David
   Barclay Moore

Suspense

Finding Mighty by Sheela Chari
Framed! by James Ponti
Greetings from Witness Protection!
   by Jake Burt
I Am Princess X by Cherie Priest
The Blackthorn Key by Kevin Sands
The Graveyard Book by Neil Gaiman
The Raft by S. A. Bodeen
Vanished! by James Ponti
Wake Up Missing by Kate Messner

Historical Fiction

Chains by Laurie Halse Anderson
Listen, Slowly by Thanhha Lai
Lucky Broken Girl by Ruth Behar
Midnight Without a Moon by Linda
   Williams Jackson
Revolution by Deborah Wiles
Riot by Walter Dean Myers
The Night Diary by Veera
   Hiranandani
The Wednesday Wars by Gary D.
   Schmidt
When My Name Was Keoko by Linda
   Sue Park

Fantasy Fiction

Circus Mirandus by Cassie Beasley
Echo by Pam Muñoz Ryan
Five Kingdoms series by Brandon
   Mull
The False Prince by Jennifer Nielsen
The Golden Compass by Philip
   Pullman
The Night Gardener by Jonathan
   Auxier
The Secret Keepers by Trenton Lee
   Stewart
The Swap by Megan Shull

Graphic Novels

*Beautiful: A Girl's Trip Through the
   Looking Glass* by Marie D'Abreo
Coraline by Neil Gaiman
*everyone's a aliebn when ur a aliebn
   too: a book* by Jomny Sun
Ghostopolis by Doug TenNapel
Nothing Can Possibly Go Wrong by
   Prudence Shen and Faith Erin
   Hicks
*Primates: The Fearless Science of
   Jane Goodall, Dian Fossey, and
   Biruté Galdikas* by Jim Ottaviani
Sunny Side Up by Jennifer Holm
Swing It, Sunny by Jennifer Holm
The Shadow Hero by Gene Luen
   Yang
Wires and Nerve by Marissa Meyer
   and Douglas Holgate

Building Empathy

A Mango-Shaped Space by Wendy Mass

Bubble by Stewart Foster

Counting by 7s by Holly Goldberg Sloan

Mockingbird by Kathryn Erskine

One for the Murphys by Lynda Mullaly Hunt

The Bridge Home by Padma Venkatraman

The Goldfish Boy by Lisa Thompson

The Science of Breakable Things by Tae Keller

The Seventh Most Important Thing by Shelley Pearsall

Sports

Babe & Me: A Baseball Card Adventure by Dan Gutman

Breakaway: Beyond the Goal by Alex Morgan

Fastbreak by Mike Lupica

Goal! The Dream Begins by Robert Rigby

Outcasts United: The Story of a Refugee Soccer Team That Changed a Town by Warren St. John

Soar by Joan Bauer

Tangerine by Edward Bloor

The Girl Who Threw Butterflies by Mick Cochrane

Dystopian Novels

Among the Hidden by Margaret Peterson Haddix

Cinder by Marissa Meyer

Legend by Marie Lu

The Giver by Lois Lowry

The Selection by Kiera Cass

The Testing by Joelle Charbonneau

Nonfiction: Engineering, Environment, and Exploration

Alien Deep: Revealing the Mysterious Living World at the Bottom of the Ocean (National Geographic Kids) by Bradley Hague

All of the Above by Shelley Pearsall

An Inconvenient Truth: The Planetary Emergency of Global Warming and What We Can Do About It by Al Gore

Blizzard! The Storm That Changed America by Jim Murphy

Bomb: The Race to Build—and Steal—the World's Most Dangerous Weapon by Steve Sheinkin

Secret Subway: The Fascinating Tale of an Amazing Feat of Engineering by Martin W. Sandler

Team Moon: How 400,000 People Landed Apollo 11 on the Moon by Catherine Thimmesh

Trash Vortex: How Plastic Pollution Is Choking the World's Oceans (Captured Science History) by Danielle Smith-Llera

The Great Fire by Jim Murphy

The Way Things Work by David Macaulay

Toys! Amazing Stories Behind Some Great Inventions by Don Wulffson

Grade 8 Book Club Bins

Realistic Fiction

Kick by Walter Dean Myers and Ross
Workman
Mexican WhiteBoy by Matt de la
Peña
Piecing Me Together by Renée
Watson
Simon vs. the Homo Sapiens Agenda
by Becky Albertalli
The Epic Fail of Arturo Zamora by
Pablo Cartaya
The House on Mango Street by
Sandra Cisneros
The Poet X by Elizabeth Acevedo
The Shepherd's Granddaughter by
Anne Laurel Carter
The Sun Is Also a Star by Nicola
Yoon

Suspense

Ashfall by Mike Mullin
*Code of Silence: Living a Lie Comes
with a Price* by Tim Shoemaker
Cover-Up: Mystery at the Super Bowl
by John Feinstein
Evil Genius by Catherine Jinks
Murder on the Orient Express by
Agatha Christie
Rebecca by Daphne du Maurier
Skink—No Surrender by Carl
Hiaasen
The Agency: A Spy in the House by
Y. S. Lee
The Face on the Milk Carton by
Caroline B. Cooney
We Were Liars by E. Lockhart

Historical Fiction

A Sky Full of Stars by Linda Williams
Jackson
Between Shades of Gray by Ruta
Sepetys
Fever 1793 by Laurie Halse Anderson
Girl in the Blue Coat by Monica
Hesse
Projekt 1065: A Novel of World War II
by Alan Gratz
Salt to the Sea by Ruta Sepetys
Soldier Boy by Keely Hutton
The Book Thief by Markus Zusak

Fantasy Fiction

Children of Blood and Bone by Tomi
Adeyemi
City of Bones by Cassandra Clare
I Am Number Four by Pittacus Lore
Renegades by Marissa Meyer
The Belles by Dhonielle Clayton
The Novice: Summoner: Book One by
Taran Matharu
The Red Queen by Victoria Aveyard
Throne of Glass by Sarah Maas
Twilight by Stephenie Meyer

Graphic Novels

Boxers and *Saints* by Gene Luen
Yang
City of Light, City of Dark by Avi
Hey Kiddo by Jarrett J. Krosoczka
I Am Alfonso Jones by Tony Medina
March series by John Lewis
Nimona by Noelle Stevenson
Persepolis: The Story of a Childhood
by Marjane Satrapi
Spill Zone by Scott Westerfeld
*The Unwanted: Stories of the Syrian
Refugees* by Don Brown
*Yummy: The Last Days of a
Southside Shorty* by G. Neri

Science Fiction

Ender's Game by Orson Scott Card
Ready Player One by Ernest Cline
Stung by Bethany Wiggins
The House of the Scorpion by Nancy
    Farmer
The Icebreaker Trilogy by Lian
    Tanner
The Martian by Andy Weir

Jason Reynolds Author Study

All American Boys
As Brave as You
Ghost
Long Way Down
Lu
Patina
Sunny
The Boy in the Black Suit

Dystopian Novels

Delirium by Lauren Oliver
Divergent by Veronica Roth
Fahrenheit 451 by Ray Bradbury
Hunger Games by Suzanne Collins
Matched by Ally Condie
Scythe by Neal Shusterman
The 5th Wave by Rick Yancey
The Maze Runner by James Dashner

Nonfiction: Resilience, Resistance, and Activism

*Ain't Nothing but a Man: My Quest
    to Find the Real John Henry* by
    Scott Reynolds Nelson with Marc
    Aronson
*Almost Astronauts: 13 Women Who
    Dared to Dream* by Tanya Lee
    Stone
Birmingham Sunday by Larry Dane
    Brimner
Fred Korematsu Speaks Up [Fighting
    for Justice Book 1] by Laura Atkins
    and Stan Yogi
*Sachiko: A Nagasaki Bomb
    Survivor's Story* by Caren Stelson
*Strike! The Farm Workers' Fight
    for Their Rights* by Larry Dane
    Brimner
The Boy Who Harnessed the Wind,
    Young Readers Edition, by William
    Kamkwamba and Bryan Mealer
*The Girl from the Tar Paper School:
    Barbara Rose Johns and the
    Advent of the Civil Rights
    Movement* by Teri Kanefield
*The Port Chicago 50: Disaster,
    Mutiny, and the Fight for Civil
    Rights* by Steve Sheinkin
*Turning Fifteen on the Road to
    Freedom: My Story of the 1965
    Selma Voting Rights March* by
    Lynda Blackmon Lowery
*We Say #NeverAgain: Reporting by
    the Parkland Student Journalists*
    edited by Melissa Falkowski and
    Eric Garner
*We Will Not Be Silent: The White
    Rose Student Resistance
    Movement That Defied Adolf Hitler*
    by Russell Freedman

3: Launching and Managing Book Clubs

Even with the excitement of organizing and setting up book clubs percolating throughout your classroom, several questions linger. How do book clubs fit into my language arts curriculum? When and where will the clubs meet? How often will they meet? What happens on the first day? What are the students doing during club meetings? And what exactly is my role as their teacher when book clubs are up and running?

When our students are in book clubs, managing them can feel like racing the clock to fit together multiple pieces of a complex puzzle. Looking back on our own experiences, we cringe when we see images of ourselves directing and disciplining our clubs. We felt like we failed our students and ourselves when a book club seemed stuck. We kept looking for more management tools, but we were searching for the wrong thing. Over the years we've realized that managing the book clubs is not about holding onto control. It's about letting go. We know that as teachers, it can be challenging to give our students ownership over their reading plans and club meetings; however, this is the recipe for success. As we breathe new life into book clubs, we need to keep our objectives about student choice and ownership in the forefront of our minds. When we do this, we find that managing book clubs will be about nurturing and empowering our students. From this stance, book clubs become positive experiences where our students fall in love with reading.

Including Book Clubs Throughout the Year

Every literacy curriculum can benefit from book clubs. They have a natural flexibility that allows teachers to customize and shape them into any calendar. Some teachers prefer to run book clubs twice a year, and others have book clubs more often. In *A Novel Approach*, Kate Roberts recommends that after we teach a whole-class reading unit, such as a study of historical fiction, we use book clubs so students can practice and transfer the skills they've

learned. Book clubs, Roberts writes, are "the perfect vehicle for helping students to practice what you have taught them about reading during the whole-class novel, only with greater independence" (2018, 124). Some teachers also recommend using book clubs as stand-alone reading units. For example, if a seventh-grade teacher knows that her students are really excited about dystopian novels such as *The Maze Runner* by James Dashner and *Divergent* by Veronica Roth, she may create a dystopian book club unit.

Our favorite time for book clubs is when our class is steeped in a writing workshop unit. This is especially true if, like us, you have a short literacy block, since book clubs allow students to practice their reading skills while freeing up more time for writing workshop. For instance, let's say we're teaching a persuasive writing unit that lasts for two weeks, and students are in goal-based book clubs where they're aiming to read a book a week. At the end of the writing unit, students will have learned about the persuasive essay and read two or more books.

Since every teacher has a different literacy schedule, fitting book clubs into literacy blocks can happen in various ways. Stephanie Seidel, a fourth-grade teacher, wisely notes that the best time for book clubs are when you know your students are ready. She shares,

At the time of the year that we delve into book clubs, the students are ready for the independence that clubs afford. They teach responsibility, cooperation, reliance, and resilience. The students delve really deeply into their reading, and, given the smaller group, those who might otherwise hold back find their voice, risk their thoughts, and contribute. As teacher-observer, you get the chance to see and hear these voices. While I perch, I hear their thinking and I am invisible to them. They become the leaders of thought. I always come out of the book club experience finding a new appreciation for my readers.

Like Stephanie, we recognize the many ways that our students are ready for the independence book clubs provide.

We invite you to begin planning for book clubs with a calendar. It is important to take into consideration your curricular calendar, reading units, and standardized testing. We recommend beginning with a three-week time span. This gives students approximately fifteen school days to read their book club book. With an average pacing of twenty pages a day, this amount of time will allow most readers to choose a book that is between 150 and 300 pages long and complete it in the required time frame. Expect book clubs reading a book at the lower page length range to read more than one book. Of course, if you are working with older students who can read more each day, you may want book clubs to last for a shorter amount of time. It is different for every class, so you and your students can decide how long it will take to read a book and what the best pacing might be. Also, you can distribute the calendar to students so they can help plan. Figure 3.1a shows a sample calendar for the month of November. The highlighted days show the weeks that book clubs will take place. A blank calendar, shown in Figure 3.1b, is available in the Online Resources.

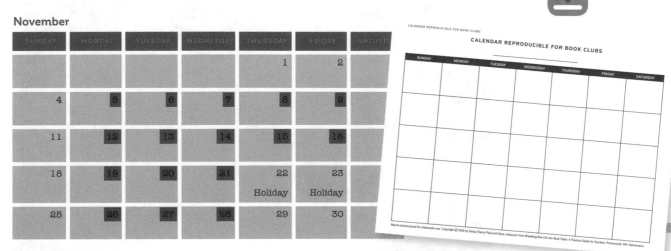

Figure 3.1a November
Calendar for Book Clubs

Figure 3.1b Calendar
Reproducible for Book Clubs

BOOK CLUB BOOKS VERSUS INDEPENDENT BOOKS

Teachers have differing opinions about whether or not students' book club book should also function as their independent reading book. Some teachers have students juggle more than one book at a time, and they have found success encouraging students to read their book club book for homework and a different independent book during class time or vice versa. Although we believe that every student should always have an independent reading book, we also recognize that our students have very full, busy lives. For this reason, we always allow our students to read their book club books during independent reading time and for nightly reading, if they choose to. This also enables students to read more pages each day, and potentially read more than one book club book in the allotted time frame.

CLUB MEETINGS

Ideally book clubs should meet at least twice a week. Mondays and Thursdays are good days for meetings since they divide the week up evenly. Having two meetings a week will keep the positive momentum going. When we first began book clubs in our classroom, we started with the Monday and Thursday model and found that our students enjoyed book clubs so

much that we increased the amount of time to three days (by including Friday). The choice is yours! It all depends on your schedule and how much time you can commit to book clubs. Some seventh- and eighth-grade teachers have found success with book club Fridays. Eighth-grader Lena appreciates "having more time to read during the week, as well as to do some blogging and writing before my club meeting on Friday." Figure 3.2 shows a snapshot of our literacy blocks and how we distribute time to make room for book clubs.

Figure 3.2
Dana's and Sonja's Schedules

DANA: I have fifty minutes for my language arts block each day. With this short amount of time, class goes by quickly! I have two nonnegotiables: My students must read and they must write! Therefore, I prioritize having fifteen minutes of independent reading each day. That leaves me with thirty-five minutes for writing and everything else. When I'm doing a book club unit, I allot 10–15 minutes for book clubs to meet three days a week. I teach my students to be efficient and use the time wisely. Also, I usually choose to do a book club unit when I'm steeped in a three-week writing workshop unit.

My schedule is:

- 15 minutes independent reading
- 10–15 minutes for book clubs (two or three times a week)
- 20–25 minutes for writing workshop

My students spend half the class on reading and half the class on writing. It is especially fun when my students are in fantasy fiction book clubs and they're writing fantasy fiction in writing workshop. The reading and writing work complement each other.

SONJA: I have an eighty-minute language arts block each day. With this amount of time, I have the flexibility to linger over texts and ideas with my students and make spur-of-the-moment changes to my schedule based on the pulse of the class. Even still, I often feel like I need more time. My two nonnegotiables are that students read and write each day. When students enter their classroom, they grab their writer's notebooks and free write for 10–15 minutes. Students read independently for 20–30 minutes. On a typical day, there are 40–45 minutes left for instruction. When book clubs are running, the writing unit often connects to what they're reading. For example, during fiction book clubs, students are working on developing a short story. During nonfiction book clubs, students are writing argumentative essays or feature articles.

My schedule:

- 10 minutes independent writing
- 20 minutes independent reading
- 20 minutes for book clubs (two to three times a week)
- 30–50 minutes for reading/writing workshop

We've created some simple weekly calendars that show you options for when book clubs might meet (see Figure 3.3). We've based these calendars on fifty-, seventy-, and ninety-minute literacy blocks with clubs that meet twice a week. Of course, you can adjust these calendars to match your class needs. The best part of book clubs is that they can be adapted to any literacy curriculum.

We love the flexibility in book clubs. You can customize your clubs to tailor-fit your literacy curriculum and routine, since they do not require a significant amount of time.

Ninety-minute literacy block

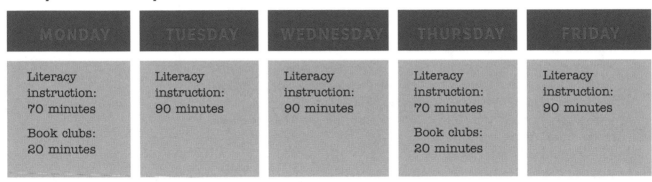

Seventy-minute literacy block

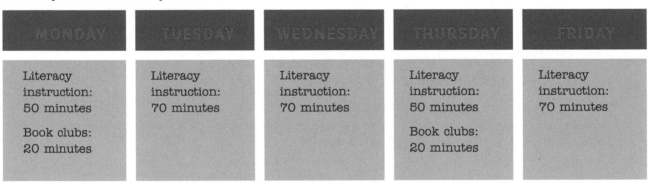

Fifty-minute literacy block

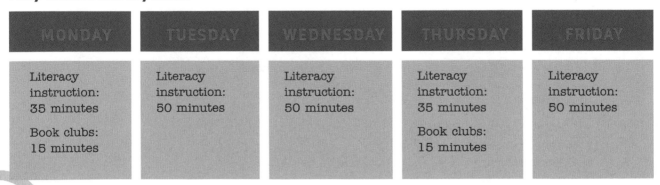

Figure 3.3 Literacy Blocks

SPACE FOR CLUBS TO MEET

Let's face it. For many of us, the physical space of our classrooms can be incredibly limiting. You might be concerned about whether you have space for multiple clubs to meet at the same time in your classroom. You'll want to anticipate this potential problem prior to the first day clubs meet. Begin by taking a good look around your classroom. You might consider locating a club in each corner of your classroom. If you have more than four book clubs, perhaps one club can meet in the center of the room. Evaluate the space right outside of your classroom. Is there one club that you can locate in the hallway close to the classroom door? We've found that many students covet this option and will rise to the challenge of behaving responsibly. Figure 3.4 shows three fifth-grade book clubs meeting in the classroom. It is important to negotiate meeting spaces with your students on or before the first day clubs meet.

The purpose of having a designated meeting location is twofold: first, it helps establish the "clubhouse" feeling you'll want students to experience, and second, it save precious time if students know exactly

Figure 3.4 Clubs
**Meeting in a Fifth-Grade
Classroom**

where to go when it's time for clubs to meet. If your classroom has individual desks, consider grouping them together for the duration of book clubs. This will also save time as students won't have to arrange the desks each time clubs meet.

One way to breathe new life into book clubs is to provide structures and access for online meetings. If this is an option, you will need to determine which digital meeting place is best for your students. For Sonja, Google Classroom and Padlet are the perfect online forums for her sixth- and seventh-grade book clubs because these are the platforms students use at school. Likewise, Dana prefers to use Kidblog and Flipgrid with her fifth graders because of students' previous experience and exposure to these platforms.

Minilesson 3.3, p. 68

Next, ask yourself what preparation, if any, students need before they use an online platform. You may want to teach your students how to have a discussion in the digital space before beginning book clubs. Your goal is to ensure that all students are comfortable working within a designated platform. Be sure to talk with your school's technology director, if needed, to determine whether students can access school accounts remotely and safely.

Practicing Great Discussions

Discussion is the heart of book clubs and is at the hub of the clubs. It is the social spark that ignites students' enthusiasm for reading. Danielle LaBella Bennett, sixth-grade special education teacher, remarks that discussions build students' interpersonal skills and comprehension and "provide students with a positive experience with books. I have seen reluctant readers enjoy reading when in book clubs and noticed increased engagement and self-esteem." As Danielle explains, discussion is the fuel that energizes book clubs.

If your students are new to or have limited experience in book clubs, they may benefit from whole-class guided practice on discussions centered around a text prior to the first club meeting. Likewise, if your students are more experienced, but have been in book clubs that have quickly unraveled, you may also consider this guided practice as a reboot. You'll want to determine whether guided practice is something that will benefit your entire class or just a small group of students. If this practice is unnecessary for your students, skip ahead to the next section, "The First Days of Book Clubs."

The purpose of guided practice is for students to learn what makes a good discussion. Too often, students think a good conversation is about controlling their behavior—raising their hands, taking turns to speak, making eye contact. Guided practice around discussions can help to debunk the conversation myths that students may believe, and helps them identify the features of authentic discussions that we want to encourage in book clubs.

For the purpose of guided practice, we recommend you use short shared texts such as short stories, poems, or digital images/texts, so the reading is quick and students can use the majority of their time to talk. While students discuss the text, walk around the classroom and listen. You may decide that your students will read these texts independently or out loud within small groups. Observe your students' conversations. Take notes about what you are seeing and hearing. What is going well? What needs improvement? As you observe, you will notice several pitfalls emerge. Resist the urge to "fix" everything you find alarming all at once. Instead, think of the quality of discussions as if they were on a continuum. We view these practice discussions as the "starting line." They are golden opportunities to notice our students' numerous strengths and to discover strategies we can teach. Overall, the most important goal in guided practice conversations is to consider our next teaching steps and help our students feel comfortable and independent. The Observation Checklist on page 63 can help you to identify next steps. On it, you'll collect artifacts and notice patterns about students' conversation over time. As you look across this tool, you'll be able to consider: Are students consistently lingering in one area or are they growing their conversations? This Observation Checklist becomes a visual for you to easily note content to coach clubs in as well as areas to celebrate clubs' growth.

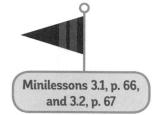

Minilessons 3.1, p. 66,
and 3.2, p. 67

After the guided practice, you may feel that students are ready to move forward and start their book clubs. Or, you may want to provide additional scaffolding and have students repeat this process with another short, engaging text, knowing that students will improve over time.

The First Days of Book Clubs

You and your students are ready for the beginning of book clubs. This is an exciting moment! Just like any other unit, you want to make sure to set the right tone from the start. There are three essential goals for the first days of book club meetings. Students must:

1) **Make reading plans.**
2) **Create written response plans.**
3) **Bond to form a strong book club identity.**

You can anticipate that the first few days of book clubs will be longer than regular club meetings because your students need time to make plans and bond. We recommend that in your first minilesson, you teach students how to form plans for their reading and provide a way that students can begin to form their club community. Teaching students how to make a plan for their written responses can happen on the first or second day depending on students' familiarity with book clubs.

PLAN TO READ

Minilesson 3.4, p. 69

Making reading plans is one of the most crucial aspects of book clubs; it's also an important lifelong reading skill. As adults, we use this time management skill often. For instance, when we are in an adult book club, we need to put ourselves on a reading schedule. We might decide to read a chapter each night before we go to sleep. That way we're finished with the book by the next monthly club meeting. Or perhaps we listen to the audiobook on our work commute each day. Making time for reading and creating effective reading plans require some backward planning, and this is a strategy students need to practice. Think about it—usually students have assignments that require them to read for a designated amount of time or pages each night. These assignments are controlled and monitored by the teacher. But book clubs that thrive are autonomous and students take ownership of their reading pace.

In book clubs, students budget their time when making plans for their reading, and these plans are flexible and adaptable to their schedules. We talked with Michelle Kaczmarek, a literacy coordinator for grades K–8, about the importance of students creating their own reading plans. Michelle shared,

> What I've seen in many classrooms is that book clubs are a great way for students to take ownership of everything they have learned in their reading instruction. It gives them the opportunity to make choices about their "readerly life"—being able to pick the book to read, creating the meeting schedule, and determining how much to read for the next session. It is amazing to see students connect with each other over this shared experience/responsibility, to be able to grow as readers, and to push each other in their thinking. While teachers are there for support, the children are the ones who drive it. They can be as creative as they want and really put their own flair into how they want the book club to run.

An increase in student engagement and ownership begins when students have the authority to choose their books and create their own plans for reading.

To help students make strong reading plans, model how they can map out their nightly reading. Using a blank calendar, students can do some simple math and plan their reading goals. Figure 3.5 shows you a sample calendar with students' nightly reading goals.

Figure 3.5 Fourth-Grade
Students' Reading Plans

Month: May

Book Title & Author: Where the Mountain Meets the Moon by Grace Lin

Monday	Tuesday	Wednesday	Thursday	Friday
	1	2	3	4
7 First Book Club Meeting pgs. 7-25 3 sticky notes	8 pgs. 26-42 3 sticky notes	9 pgs. 43-59 3 sticky notes	10 Book Club Meeting pgs. 60-78 write reflection in reading notebook	11
14 Book Club Meeting pgs. 79-96 5 sticky notes	15 pgs. 97-114 3 sticky notes	16 pgs. 115-131 5 sticky notes	17 Book Club Meeting pgs. 132-159 choose BEST sticky notes	18
21 Book Club Meeting pgs. 160-181 5 sticky notes	22 pgs. 182-202 5 sticky notes	23 pgs. 203-223 5 sticky notes	24 Book Club Meeting pgs. 224-244 5 sticky notes	25
28 Book Club Meeting pgs. 246-End!	29	30	31 Book Club Celebration!	

Eloise, a fourth-grade student noted, "My favorite part about book clubs was how we could read whatever we wanted to. We could decide to read whatever number of pages a night we wanted to. I like deciding my own homework, especially when I have piano after school." When students create their own reading plans, they feel empowered and independent as readers, and this helps create a strong culture of reading in our classrooms.

PLAN TO WRITE

Students feel equally independent and empowered with opportunities to create their own written response plans. We encourage our book clubs to create a few written responses each week, and here's what we've noticed: (1) We've never seen our students so excited to have homework assignments. (2) They're more invested in the quality of their written responses when they know they will be sharing them with their club. (3) It helps create a stronger community of readers and learners. Fifth-grade students in The Library Wizards book club savored the opportunity to create written response plans so much that they challenged themselves to think of creative assignments. Some included making their own annotation symbols (one was a duck vomiting, which meant something was *really* gross), taking on different characters' perspective and writing diary entries from their points of view, and creating play scripts so they could act out their favorite scenes during recess.

Minilesson 3.5, p. 70

Before students make written response plans, it is important to brainstorm a list of possibilities and set guidelines for amounts of writing. Make sure your students can refer to this list whenever they need to. You may decide to hang it in the classroom, have your students record it in their reading notebook, send it out as a Google Classroom Announcement, share it as a Google Doc, and so on. For some teachers, the priority for book clubs is reading; therefore, written response work is shorter in length. For other teachers, and for older readers, there may be an expectation for lengthier pieces of writing. However, we want to urge you to keep the focus on reading.

PLAN TO FORM STRONG BOOK CLUB IDENTITIES

It's essential for clubs to form a community and create a unique identity. Think back to your own experiences on a sports team or in a summer camp. Can you hear the corny cheers you used to say with your friends? Do you remember the team names or mascots you made up? Can you picture the matching athletic uniforms you wore and the posters you created? These activities helped bring you together as a team or a cabin. Students can create the same experience in their book clubs, and when they do it well, these clubs may last well beyond the classroom. We've had book clubs make such tight bonds that students kept their clubs going on their own— meeting at recess or on the weekends. Some clubs have even had reunions with each other after the school year is over. Kyrie, a sixth grader, said, "I really bonded with my book club. We bonded over the books we were reading and our opinions about them. We have a lot of memories together." To develop strong bonds, determining core values becomes integral to the strength of their book club. We can help students make book clubs sacred by asking them to think and talk about their beliefs: What do they believe will make this the best book club ever? What are the qualities that are important to them that they will honor and uphold in this club? How can they work together as a team to achieve their goals? A book club can be like a nation of its own. It can operate as a dictatorship, ruled by a teacher or a member of the club, or it can be a democracy where each voice matters. We won't pretend that democracy is easy. However, we can challenge students to identify how they'd like to feel in the book club world they create. Common responses include respected, safe, and valued. In essence, students create their own culture and protocols that become a compass for how they treat one another. Routine reflection on these core values helps each book club to stay on course.

We recommend you include one short community-forming activity during the first two or three book club meetings. For example, students can create their club name on Day 1, a banner or Padlet on Day 2, and a list of Club Goals on Day 3. These short bonding activities help sustain the momentum that's been building for book clubs, and students feel more engaged when they have ownership over their club.

Club Names

No matter the age group, book clubs should always have names. This is an important first step for book clubs when they are forming their own identities. We recommend that clubs create their name at the first club meeting. Some clubs' names will have great puns and others will reveal students' interests and details about themselves (see Figure 3.6). We've had everything from the Flying Pages to the Pink Panthers and even the Bare Minimums.

Minilesson 3.6, p. 71

Figure 3.6 The Rapid Readers' Club Sign

Club Banners, Flags, or Mascots

We've found that making a banner, flag, or mascot for their club is a great way for students to get into the book club spirit! Banners or flags can be positioned near the clubs' meeting spaces or on a bulletin board. Figure 3.7 shows the Library Wizards' club members proudly showing off their banner. As Tricia, a fifth-grade student and proud member of the Library Wizards said, "What I like about my book club is how much fun I have while I read with my team. I think my club has a great imagination and our banner was just really us." Club mascots are especially effective with younger students. They are excited to have a stuffed animal or a picture of the mascot that attends each club meeting. Younger readers enjoy reading aloud to the mascot during club meetings or including the mascot in their discussions. This is a fun way to get younger readers engaged and feeling connected to their club community.

Figure 3.7 The Library Wizards' Club Banner

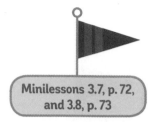

Minilessons 3.7, p. 72,
and 3.8, p. 73

Club Constitutions or Club Goals

You might invite students to create a club constitution or club goals so they can lay out very basic guidelines for themselves. Although some clubs may not need this type of scaffold, other clubs may need it so all their members know what is expected. For instance, students may have strong opinions about whether or not club members can read ahead, or how they should proceed if a student is not doing their reading.

Group Photo

Taking a club photo and hanging it somewhere in the classroom or posting it on book club blogs is a great way to help clubs bond. You can invite students to hold up a sign that says their club name or a flag with their club mascot. Of course, instead of saying "Cheese!" you'll ask students to say, "Read!"

Digital Tools

We love using blogs and Padlets with our books clubs. These tools allow students to create a unique club identity within a digital space, and these spaces can be shared with the whole class, across classes, and even across schools. We've found great success using blogging with our students because it fuels discussion and helps them to create a strong book club identity. Fifth-grader Chrissy was a quiet member of her book club, the Fantastic Four. She rarely spoke during her group's in-class conversations. However, she loved writing on her group's blog, and she came up with many imaginative ideas for how to use Kidblog. As teachers, we know that our students often discover fun and innovative ways to use technology. Chrissy created the idea of "Stickies Selfies." She encouraged her book club to snap a photo of their best sticky notes to share on the blog. This idea fueled her group's motivation to make strong sticky notes, and Chrissy helped organize the Stickies Selfies on her group's blog as shown in Figure 3.8. This was just one of Chrissy's many creative ideas that helped strengthen her club's identity and community.

Figure 3.8 Fifth-grade students use Kidblog to display "Stickies Selfies."

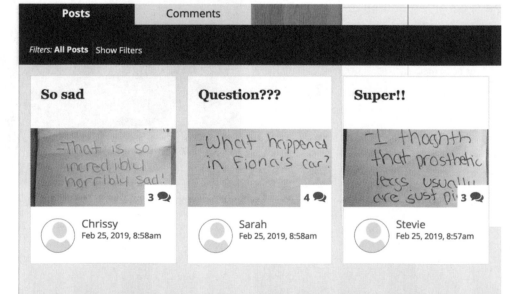

School Newspaper / School Book Blog / Library Display

Some schools publish a newspaper or blog with a section devoted to book recommendations. This is a great place for book clubs to submit an article or post about the books they're reading. Also, librarians are often looking for new book display ideas, and they might be interested in partnering with book clubs to create a new display.

Making Book Clubs Go! Observing, Coaching, and Assessing

One of the most common concerns teachers have about book clubs is the role of the teacher. Once the clubs are off and running, now what? What exactly does the teacher do beyond circulating between the clubs? Observation is a key component. Think of your role throughout book clubs, but particularly during the initial meetings, as that of a researcher. As such you will be observing and collecting artifacts that help you make sense of what's happening in each club. Artifacts include quick jottings of what you hear students saying, number of pages read, students who are (and aren't) prepared with materials, types of written responses students are doing, how technology is being used to support student work, and so on. You might also observe that clubs are having difficulties with planning. Some students, for example, may be too ambitious and therefore make unrealistic goals for reading and written responses. They may be setting themselves up to experience unnecessary stress. Other clubs may be reading at a pace that will cause the reading to drag along for weeks or months. Perhaps you notice that some students are unprepared with materials or just haven't done the work the club assigned and agreed upon. What seems to be going on with these students? Getting to the bottom of this is imperative for the club to thrive.

In Figure 3.9, Dana uses the Organization and Planning Graphic Organizer to take the pulse of her clubs that are up and running. The Organization and Planning Graphic Organizer in Figure 3.10 (available in the Online Resources) can help you to collect data and to essentially take the pulse of each book club now that they're up and running.

Teachers can ask themselves many questions as they make observations throughout the duration of book clubs. What seems to be working well? What issues are emerging? For example, one of your first observations may be about the discussion. What are students saying? How are they speaking to one another? Are some students not speaking at all? How are students reacting and responding to what is said? And of course, you'll make observations about reading comprehension. Are students understanding the text? Are they using literary elements to elevate their interpretations? Is text evidence being provided to support their claims?

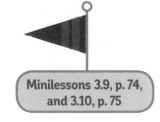

Minilessons 3.9, p. 74,
and 3.10, p. 75

ORGANIZATION AND PLANNING GRAPHIC ORGANIZER

ORGANIZATION AND PLANNING GRAPHIC ORGANIZER

Club Name: _Cover to Cover_

Club Members: _Carla, Kevin, Shawn, Sarah S._

Text(s): _Blended by Sharon Draper_

Organization and Planning
Are clubs demonstrating routines and implementing strategies that make book clubs go?

OBSERVATIONS	COACHING PLANS
Club Preparation Are students coming prepared to the meetings with the materials they need? 11/12 → Yes! Ⓚ forgot book but read. 11/15 → Ⓚ forgot book.	11/15 → Talked to Ⓚ privately.
Reading Plans Are students meeting their goals for how many pages they plan to read each night and are they adjusting them when needed? 11/12 → Club reviewed plans. Made a few adjustments. 11/15 → Nightly reading plans overwhelming.	11/15 → Students revise their calendar. Made realistic plans.
Writing Plans Are students responding to text(s) in writing using a variety of methods such as sticky notes, reading notebooks, blogs, etc.? 11/12 → Sticky notes only. 11/15 → Several blog entries on padlet about characters.	11/12 → Discussed other written response items. Ex. RN, blogging. Club excited to try blogging. 11/15 → Worked on new ways to discuss texts. Ex. setting, conflict
Club Culture Are students creating and nurturing a book club community that encourages the joy of reading? 11/12 → Set up blog page. 11/15 → Ⓒ seems quiet. Having a hard time sharing ideas.	11/15 → Try silent chart chat?

May be photocopied for classroom use. Copyright © 2019 by Sonja Cherry-Paul and Dana Johansen from *Breathing New Life into Book Clubs: A Practical Guide for Teachers*. Portsmouth, NH: Heinemann.

Figure 3.9 (left)
Organization and Planning Graphic Organizer, Completed Version

Figure 3.10 (below)
Organization and Planning Graphic Organizer, Blank Version

ORGANIZATION AND PLANNING GRAPHIC ORGANIZER

ORGANIZATION AND PLANNING GRAPHIC ORGANIZER

What, if any, methods are they using to repair misunderstandings? Are they making noteworthy critiques of characters, issues, the author, themselves? The observations we make inform the coaching that we'll customize for each book club. The Observation Checklist allows us to keep track of what's happening in each club. For example, as we look across the artifacts we've collected, we might notice that multiple clubs are experiencing challenges with analyzing character traits. Therefore, we might pull those students together and teach a minilesson that addresses this pitfall. But most of the instruction that occurs during book clubs will be in the form of coaching. See Figure 3.11 for a completed Observation Checklist of a fifth-grade book club. See Figure 3.12 for a blank form, available in the Online Resources.

In our book club components, we've used a sports analogy to emphasize that when the game is happening, or in this case, when the students are in their clubs, we'll need to provide quick, five-minute or less coaching tips that are designed to give students a strategy or the clarification they need to get back on track. Remember, based on our English or language arts schedules, we may not have the luxury of twenty minutes or more for book clubs. And if our overarching goal is for students to become lifelong lovers of reading, taking away the time for students to read and discuss and replacing this with lengthy, complex lessons will not help us to achieve this goal. Instead, consider: What can you do in a few minutes to elevate the work of this book club right now? And we must also remember that we'll have the duration of the book club unit as well as subsequent book club units occurring in the year to continue to address our observations.

OBSERVATION CHECKLIST

OBSERVATION CHECKLIST

As you listen in on a club's discussion, record your observations in the checklist below. Over time, you may notice patterns in the club's discussion topics and how members utilize reading comprehension strategies. In order to teach the club new paths for conversation as well as comprehension tools, see the minilessons noted in the far right column.

Club name: _Cover to Cover_

What are students talking about?

Students are talking about . . .	DATE 11/12	DATE 11/15	DATE 11/19	DATE 11/21	DATE 11/26	MINILESSONS
off-task topics	✓	✓			✓	4.1, 4.3, 4.8, 4.10
a summary of what they read	✓	✓	✓			4.2, 4.3, 4.6
questions about vocabulary, characters, or the plot	✓	✓	✓	✓	✓	5.3, 5.7, 5.11, 5.15
characters' traits, motivations, relationships, or conflicts	✓	✓	✓	✓	✓	5.3, 5.4, 5.15
connections between texts				✓	✓	5.6, 5.8
connections to their own lives or the world			✓	✓		5.6, 5.8
predictions		✓				5.10, 5.11
literary elements (theme, symbolism, figurative language, etc.)				✓	✓	5.6, 5.12, 5.13
author's purpose				✓	✓	5.8, 5.11
Other:						

What discussion/reading comprehension strategies are they using?

Students are . . .	DATE 11/12	DATE 11/15	DATE 11/19	DATE 11/21	DATE 11/26	MINILESSONS
posing questions	✓	✓	✓			4.1, 4.5, 5.7, 5.10
summarizing; retelling			✓			4.1, 4.3, 4.4, 5.1, 5.2, 5.7
rereading; finding text evidence			✓	✓		4.7, 5.4, 5.7, 5.10
annotating to illuminate their thinking	✓	✓	✓			4.7, 5.10
analyzing to determine significance; critiquing a text				✓	✓	4.4, 4.9, 5.5, 5.6, 5.8, 5.9
Other:						

continues

Figure 3.11 (left)
**Observation Checklist,
Completed Version**

Figure 3.12 (below)
**Observation Checklist,
Blank Version**

OBSERVATION CHECKLIST

OBSERVATION CHECKLIST

As you listen in on a club's discussion, record your observations in the checklist below. Over time, you may notice patterns in the club's discussion topics and how members utilize reading comprehension strategies. In order to teach the club new paths for conversation as well as comprehension tools, see the minilessons noted in the far right column.

Club name

What are students talking about?

If we're being honest, sometimes a club just doesn't work out. Perhaps a student grouping was an epic failure and no amount of intervening made things better. Perhaps students tried their best, but for reasons much too nuanced to tease out, things never really got off the ground. Without anger, frustration, or "book club shaming," we simply need to make a new plan. And perhaps the plan is for students within the club to finish reading in partnerships or even independently if necessary. Say to students, "I value you and your growth as readers so much that we have to change course to make things better for all of you." And we continue to provide the coaching all students need—whether they're in a book club, in a book partnership, or working independently. Because all students, regardless of method, are part of the clubhouse of reading.

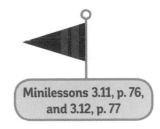

Minilessons 3.11, p. 76, and 3.12, p. 77

Breathing New Life into Launching and Managing Book Clubs

Donalyn Miller, author of _The Book Whisperer_, inspires us with her unconditional love and support for all readers. She writes, "No matter what kind of reader you are, know that I value you and welcome you here" (2009, 6). These words echo in our minds as we endeavor to reimagine ways of creating book clubs that are independent, vibrant reading communities.

We'd love for you to pause here and reflect on ways that you can breathe new life into book clubs. Whether you're beginning book clubs for the first time or looking for ways to refresh or elevate your clubs, we encourage you to consider how the following ideas can play a role.

Chapter Three Resources at a Glance

IDEAS	SPECIFICS	RESOURCES
Consider where and when book clubs fit in! Begin with a three-week time span, which includes fifteen school days for students to read as well as meet two times per week.	*When will book clubs occur in my literacy curriculum and how often should they meet?* Try book clubs: • After a whole class novel • As a stand-alone unit • During a writing unit	**Calendar for book clubs** p. 49 **Sample literacy block schedules** p. 52
Determine designated spaces for book clubs to meet! Establish a "clubhouse" feeling as well as maximize time by negotiating meeting spaces with students before the first day clubs meet.	*Where will all of the books clubs meet?* Locate several options such as: • Each corner of the classroom • The hallway or alcove nearby • Online meetings	**Lesson 3.3: Blogging Guidelines and Digital Citizenship** p. 68
Practice discussions about texts! Provide time for guided-practice on text-based discussions prior to the first club meeting.	*How can I help students to determine characteristics of good discussions?* Observe how students read and discuss a short engaging text (digital, poem, short story) and note their strengths and areas for improvement.	**Lesson 3.1: Fueling Discussions with Digital Texts** p. 66 **Lesson 3.2: Revving Up Talk Through Practice Discussions** p. 67
Assist students as they make reading and writing book club plans! Model the ways students can plan out their reading as well as several ways they can develop written responses.	*How can I support students in making (and keeping) strong reading and writing plans?* Demonstrate options such as: • Map out nightly reading • Brainstorm and post written response possibilities	**Lesson 3.4: Making Strong Reading Plans** p. 69 **Lesson 3.5: Making Strong Written Response Plans** p. 70 **Lesson 3.9: Honoring Club Commitments** p. 74 **Lesson 3.10: Revising Reading Plans** p. 75
Help book clubs bond! Encourage students to identify the practices that will help them work together and accomplish their goals.	*How can I help students cultivate an environment where each club member feels safe, valued, and respected?* Get students into the "clubhouse" spirit by inviting them to create: • Club names • Club banners, flags, or mascots • Club constitutions or club goals • Club photos • Digital space	**Lesson 3.6: Creating Club Names** p. 71 **Lesson 3.7: Writing Club Constitutions** p. 72 **Lesson 3.8: Setting Club Goals** p. 73
Observe, coach, assess! Collect artifacts that help you to make sense of what's happening in each book club.	*What is my role as the teacher during book clubs?* Collect data that help you to design the instruction clubs need to thrive.	**Organization and Planning Graphic Organizer** p. 62 **Observation Checklist** p. 63

PATHWAY MINILESSONS

3.1

Fueling Discussions with Digital Texts

Pitfall: Club members are experiencing challenges with discussions.

Pathway: Consider using a short, engaging digital text to ignite discussion and fuel students' understanding of what makes a good conversation. Many special education and English language learner teachers find digital texts particularly effective when working with a wide variety of students. You can begin by selecting a photograph, advertisement, or short video clip. If you decide to use a photograph, we recommend images of animals, scenic views, or intriguing objects. You can see examples of these in Figure 3.13.

Begin your lesson as a whole class to closely examine the digital text. Ask students to list any ideas, questions, or responses they have about the digital text. Then, create small, random groups of students, and invite students to engage in a discussion about the digital text in their small groups. There should be a buzz of conversation in your classroom. When you come back together as a whole class, discuss and list all the different responses to the digital text. Remind students that the buzz that just occurred is what we're striving for in our book club discussions.

Figure 3.13
Three Digital Text
Examples

Revving Up Talk Through Practice Discussions

Pitfall: Club discussions may feel rigid at first, and students may need to practice having authentic conversations.

Pathway: Begin by selecting a short, highly engaging text. Create small, random groups of students. These are *not* the actual book clubs, but practice groups.

Provide copies of the text and read it aloud or silently as a whole class. When students are finished, have them write or list any ideas, questions, or responses they have to the text. Invite students to engage in a discussion about the text in their small groups.

Observe your students while they are talking, but do not intervene in their discussions. Reconvene the class, and ask students, "Based on the experience you've just had with your peers, what are some features of a good discussion?" (Some ideas may include sharing different ideas, asking questions, listening, feeling heard, wanting to talk more.) Together, create a chart titled What Are Features of a Good Discussion? See Figure 3.14 for an example.

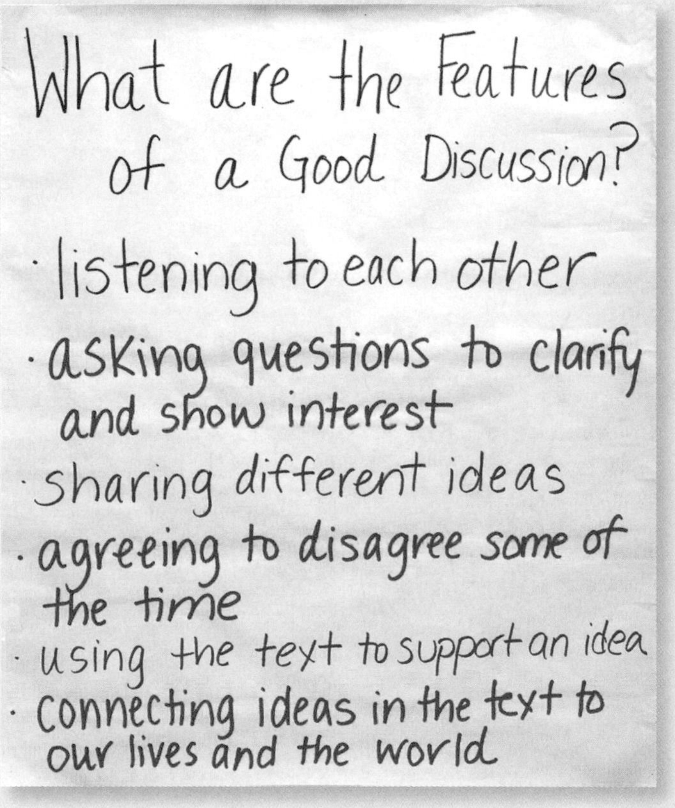

> What are the Features of a Good Discussion?
>
> · listening to each other
> · asking questions to clarify and show interest
> · sharing different ideas
> · agreeing to disagree some of the time
> · using the text to support an idea
> · connecting ideas in the text to our lives and the world

Figure 3.14 What Are the Features of a Good Discussion? Chart

3.3

Blogging Guidelines and Digital Citizenship

Pitfall: Students are starting to blog, but they need guidance about digital citizenship and respectful blogging practices.

Pathway: It doesn't matter if you have novice or advanced bloggers. All students benefit from a minilesson on digital citizenship when blogging during book clubs. After you introduce students to the blogging platform, the following steps can help them throughout the book club.

First, talk to students about the purpose of using a blog—it will help students bond, enhance their discussions, and bring positive, fun energy to their club.

Next, talk to students about the importance of being a respectful blogger. You might consider creating a chart, such as Figure 3.15a, that reminds them of the rules.

For some teachers, it is important to create a blog post checklist, like the one in Figure 3.15b, so students understand the writing expectations.

Consider doing a practice round of writing blogs before you use them in book clubs. For example, you might add a blogging component to Lessons 3.1 and 3.2.

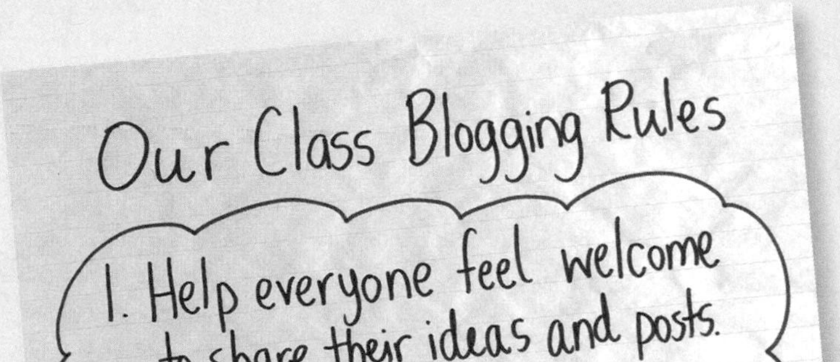

Figure 3.15a (left) Our Class Blogging Rules

Figure 3.15b (below) Blog Post Checklist

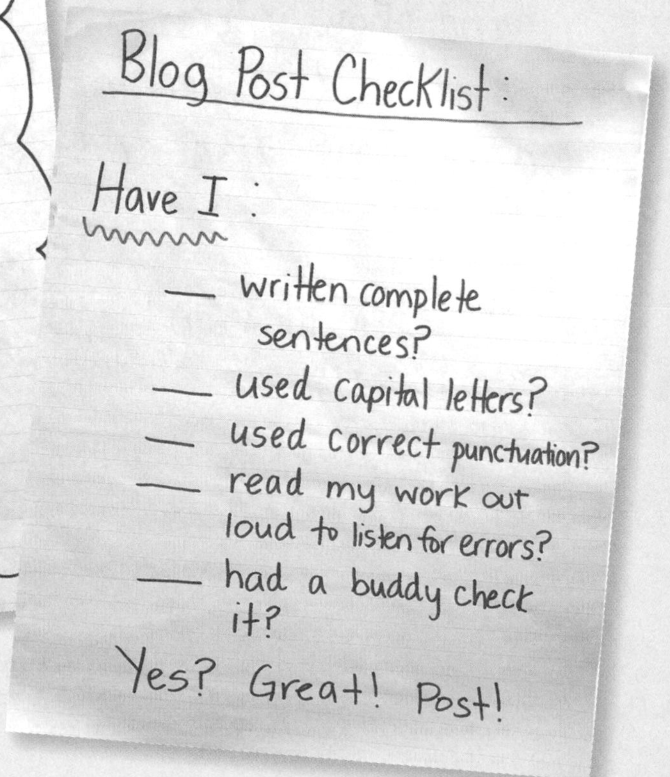

Our Class Blogging Rules

1. Help everyone feel welcome to share their ideas and posts.

2. Write positive feedback.

3. Be specific in your feedback and ideas.

4. Present your work maturely.

5. Check your writing for capitalization and spelling.

Blog Post Checklist:

Have I :

— written complete sentences?

— used capital letters?

— used correct punctuation?

— read my work out loud to listen for errors?

— had a buddy check it?

Yes? Great! Post!

Making Strong Reading Plans

3.4

Pitfall: Club members need a model for how to make effective reading plans.

Pathway: Convene your whole class or individual book club to talk about the importance of making reading plans. Use yourself as a model. Explain that when you know the length of time you have to read a book, you look at a calendar and plan your nightly reading. This involves a bit of math so you can estimate how many pages you should read each night to finish the book in the allotted time.

Hold up a calendar. This calendar should be the one you intend to hand out to your students. It should identify the book club unit as well as the club meeting dates. See the sample calendar in Figure 3.16.

Empower students to take ownership of their clubs, which includes working together to set reasonable reading plans. Also, remind students that reading plans are flexible and can be adjusted at each club meeting if students find they are not working out.

Figure 3.16 Sample Student Google Doc Calendar

Month: October
Text: <u>Front Desk</u> by Kelly Yang

Sunday	Monday	Tuesday	Wednesday	Thursday	Friday	Saturday
	1	2	3	4	5	6
7	8	9	10	11	12	13
14	15 1st Meeting Pgs. 8-28	16 Pgs. 29-48	17 Pgs. 49-72 Blog Post	18 2nd Meeting Pgs. 73-93	19 Pgs. 94-112	20 Pgs. 113-139
21	22 3rd Mtg. Pgs. 140-164	23 Pgs. 165-187 Blog Post	24 Pgs. 187-211	25 4th Mtg. Pgs. 212-239	26 Pgs. 240-265	27 Read to the end!
28	29 Talk and start new book!!!	30	31	1	2	3

3.5

Making Strong Written Response Plans

Pitfall: Club members need to see the possibilities and potential of written response work.

Pathway: Remember, writing plans do not need to be onerous, nor do they need to be assigned as homework. They can be fun and creative, and they can happen during book club meetings. The most important thing is that our students learn how to reflect on their reading and have an opportunity to construct their own interpretations of the text.

To best support your students, pull together the entire class or an individual book club. Talk about the ways written response strengthens their ideas and discussions about a text. Then, brainstorm ideas for written responses such as:

- sticky note annotations
- blog posts
- Stickies Selfies (see Figure 3.8)
- diary entries
- questions to the author or characters
- free responses.

Some book clubs may assign themselves three sticky notes a night, and other clubs may write entire fan fiction chapters. It really depends on each club, and what works best for the students in that club.

In Figure 3.17, you can see how one book club member used Padlet to blog about *Out of My Mind* by Sharon Draper. Under the blog post, you can see fellow club members reply.

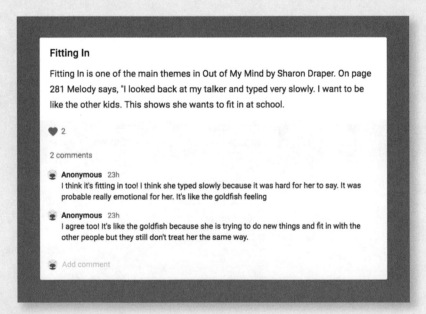

Figure 3.17 Student Blog Post and Reply About *Out of My Mind* by Sharon Draper

Creating Club Names

3.6

Pitfall: Club members are mired in arguments over their club name and need quick tips for creating catchy book club names.

Pathway: Give your students three or four sample club names. Usually, clubs only need a few examples to move themselves forward. Figure 3.18 shows club names on a bulletin board.

You can also provide the following five quick tips for creating a catchy club name.

1) Make a club name that uses reading words. Think: *bookworms*, *pages*, and so on.

2) Create a club name that uses confident, strong words like *rock stars*, *awesome*, *best*, and so on.

3) Make an acronym using the first letter of every club member's first name to form a new word.

4) Think of a club name based on the title or content of the text the club is reading.

5) Think of a favorite author or literary saying.

If your students are especially inspired, they can also create a motto such as "We are the Page Turners. We have the need to read!"

Figure 3.18 Book Club Signs on Bulletin Board

3.7

Writing Club Constitutions

Pitfall: Club members need to establish core values that help their club run smoothly.

Pathway: Begin by talking to your whole class or individual club about what a club constitution is. Show a model club constitution (like the one shown in Figure 3.19) and talk to your students about what they may want to include in their constitution. Provide two or three guiding questions: What's going to make this the best club ever? What are our responsibilities as club members? What commitments will we make to respect each other's growth as we read and discuss texts?

Be sure to remind students to keep it simple. There's no need to have more than five items. Figure 3.19 is an example of a fifth-grade book club constitution.

Check in with each club individually to monitor the progress they are making. Redirect students if the content on their club constitution feels like it is targeting a specific student's work habits, if it feels punitive, or if it feels unreasonable. Book clubs are meant to be flexible, relaxed, and enjoyable. Also, provide options for where each club will post its constitution to refer to it in the future.

> ## The Page Turners
>
> We, the members of The Page Turners, plan to negotiate our ideas and to have an open mind about other people's opinions. Even if one of us feels one way and another feels differently, our book club won't work if we don't cooperate.
>
> When we assign ourselves reading, we will read those pages, so that everyone is on the same page ⅂ If someone doesn't read the decided pages, the whole book club is punished because it slows everyone down to wait for that person.
>
> If one of us tries to slack off and let other people do all the work, that person won't be learning anything, and it is unfair to our clubmates.
>
> Our book club will work together as a team!

Figure 3.19 Club Constitution

Setting Club Goals

Pitfall: Clubs need to set reasonable reading and written response goals to identify their hopes and dreams for themselves as readers.

Pathway: Begin this discussion with either the whole class or an individual book club. Talk to students about setting reading and written response goals. Model this for students by showing them a list of goals from a former book club. If you haven't done this before, create a sample list for your students like the one in Figure 3.20.

These goals are proactive, positive, and upbeat. For example, one club might have the following goals: "Try reading a new genre," "Stretch our conversations," "Increase our reading stamina."

Watch out for clubs that are making lists of rules. Redirect students by reminding them that they are setting goals that will act as their hopes and dreams for the book club to achieve. Visit all the clubs to check on their progress. Provide options for where each club can keep these goals handy.

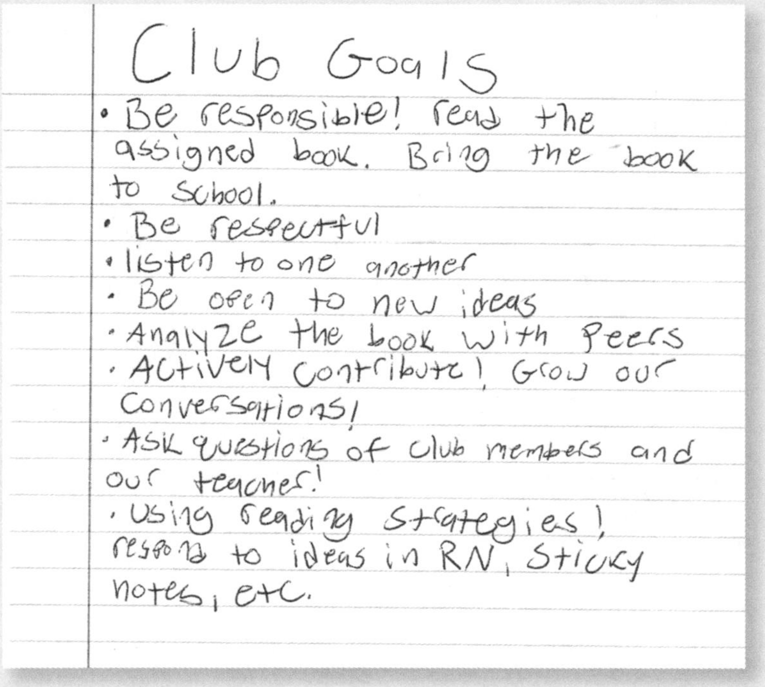

Club Goals
- Be responsible! Read the assigned book. Bring the book to school.
- Be respectful
- listen to one another
- Be open to new ideas
- Analyze the book with peers
- Actively contribute! Grow our conversations!
- Ask questions of club members and our teacher!
- Using reading strategies! respond to ideas in RN, sticky notes, etc.

Figure 3.20 Club Goals

3.9

Honoring Club Commitments

Pitfall: It is challenging for members to complete agreed-upon club reading and written responses.

Pathway: Speak privately with individual students who are not honoring their club commitments and help students get back on track.

However, if you notice that a large group of students are not honoring their book club commitments, talk to the whole class or individual book clubs about the commitments they made in their club constitutions.

You might say, "The best part about book clubs is that as a group you can make your own goals and lead your own discussions. As we've learned from reading Spider-Man comics, 'with great power there must also come—great responsibility'. This means that we must honor our commitments to our clubs. Today I want you to review your club constitution, so that everyone is on the same page. If any goals need to change, make those adjustments today. Today will be a fresh start. I'm going to check in with your club(s) to hear about your ideas for moving forward together." Figure 3.21 shows a fifth-grade student's revisions to her club's constitution.

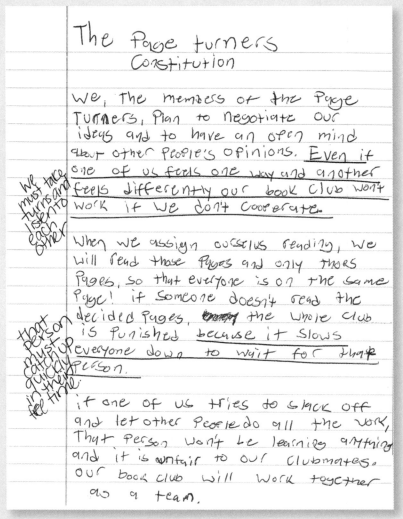

Figure 3.21 Student Revising Club Constitution

Revising Reading Plans

Pitfall: Although clubs have used a calendar to make reading plans, they are having a difficult time adjusting their reading plans as needed.

Pathway: Part of making strong reading plans is the ability to shift the plans as needed. At times, we will see book clubs that are inflexible about their plans or unable to make plans that are reasonable. Therefore, students will need to learn how to adjust their plans for the benefit of all members of the club.

Work with an individual book club on members' reading plans. Teach students to take into consideration their varied and full lives. Questions students can consider when making reading plans are:

1) What projects and assessments do we have coming up in other classes?

2) What's going on outside of school (sports, recitals, family celebrations, etc.)?

When students begin to map out their schedules, they are more likely to create reading plans they can stick to and also adjust when needed. Figure 3.22 shows a student's revisions to her reading plans.

Month: May

Book Title & Author: Where the Mountain Meets the Moon by Grace Lin

Monday	Tuesday	Wednesday	Thursday	Friday
	1	2	3	4
7 First Book Club Meeting pgs. 7–25 3 sticky notes	8 pgs. 26–42 3 sticky notes 97–131	9 pgs. 43–59 3 sticky notes No reading	10 Book Club Meeting pgs. 60–78 write reflection in reading notebook	11
14 Book Club Meeting pgs. 79–96 5 sticky notes	15 pgs. 97–114 5 sticky notes Project	16 pgs. 115–131 5 sticky notes Project	17 Book Club Meeting pgs. 132–159 Choose BEST sticky notes	18
21 Book Club Meeting pgs. 160–181 5 sticky notes	22 pgs. 182–202 5 sticky notes	23 pgs. 203–223 5 sticky notes	24 Book Club Meeting pgs. 224–244 5 sticky notes	25
28 Book Club Meeting pgs. 246–End!	29	30	31 Book Club Celebration!	

Figure 3.22 Student Revising Reading Plans on Calendar

3.11 Rekindling Enthusiasm for Book Clubs

Pitfall: The momentum for book clubs has fizzled, and clubs need a resurgence of energy and enthusiasm.

Pathway: Try one of the following ways to ignite momentum for book clubs again:

1) Try one of the strategies from Chapter 2 about drumming up excitement for book clubs.

2) Bring in a guest to talk about their experiences in a book club. This could be a former student, administrator, or visitor, for example.

3) Incorporate technology. Have your students compose a tweet to their book club author. Send the tweet to the author. They may respond! Figure 3.23 shows students' tweets.

4) Have a mid–book club celebration. Use one of the ideas in Chapter 6 to celebrate.

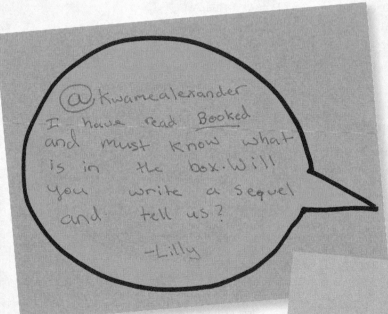

Figure 3.23 Connecting with Authors via Twitter

Abandoning the Book and Changing Course

Pitfall: Sometimes book club members realize that their club book is not a good fit for them and want to abandon their book (see Figure 3.24).

Pathway: There are two occasions when students might need to change course in book clubs. Sometimes students will ask if they can switch book clubs because they feel that the book the club is reading is too challenging for them or they simply are not connecting with it. Other times, an entire book club may read the first two chapters of the book, and all the members agree that the book was not what they envisioned. They may ask to switch books.

In our experience, these scenarios happen infrequently, but when they do, it is important to help students find a book that works for them. Above all, we want our students to have a positive book club experience and grow as readers. It's valuable for all readers to advocate for themselves and learn when to put a book down. When this happens, our work is to help students navigate their options:

- The book club members may select a new book for their club.
- An individual club member can switch clubs to read a book that's a better fit.
- We can create partnerships within a club where students may read different texts but have whole-club conversations around characters, theme, and main ideas.
- Sometimes, students may choose to read independently during book club time because this, in fact, is the best choice for them as readers.

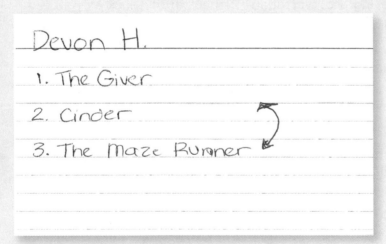

Figure 3.24 Student's Revised Ranked List

4: Lighting the Fire of Discussion

Have you ever listened in on a small group of children having a conversation? Perhaps in the back of your minivan, at your kitchen table, or in the cafeteria. Or even in your classroom once you've walked away from a group. When a group of children communicate, it's loud. There's laughter, repetition, and talk that tumbles over each other at times. And there's multitasking. When kids are talking, they are typically doing something: tossing a hat, ball, or pencil into the air; drawing or writing; using a smart device or laptop to verify or build upon an idea. Within these seemingly chaotic conditions, the children somehow manage not to miss a beat. When children gather, there's energy, movement, noise.

Although we can readily observe and accept the authentic ways in which children communicate in spaces beyond our classrooms, this isn't always valued inside of them. We become alarmed when this occurs under our watchful eyes. We think our students can't possibly be learning! So we try to subdue these behaviors by providing rules and structures that discourage them. It's no wonder some students dislike book clubs when

these decisions are imposed upon them. It's no wonder some teachers avoid book clubs in the classroom altogether when their fear of chaos is so strong.

Abbe Hocherman, literacy specialist for grades 5–8, reflects on student book club discussions. She explains,

> I have found it's hard to get used to letting go of control. At first I felt that if I was not the one posing the questions, then the "important bits" of a book would not be uncovered. I think setting up the structures for deep thinking and genuine productive talk takes time, practice, and opportunity to fail a little bit. It's hard to leave space in the class for these things. I struggle with finding the right balance of enough scaffolds and structures for kids to lift their thinking without squashing their genuine curiosity and enjoyment of the experience. In my book clubs, there have been times when conversations went silent. The students weren't sure how to sustain the talk in a genuine way. I had to shine a light on that and then spend time gearing instruction to that point. I also struggled with making the talk feel genuine but also making the students feel accountable to the richness of the conversation.

Abbe's concerns echo those of many educators.

With some guidance, students are able to engage in rich conversations that are similar to those that occur in adult book clubs. So what can we learn from adult conversations? There are several noes. No roles. No rules about taking turns. No requirements for how long to stay on a topic.

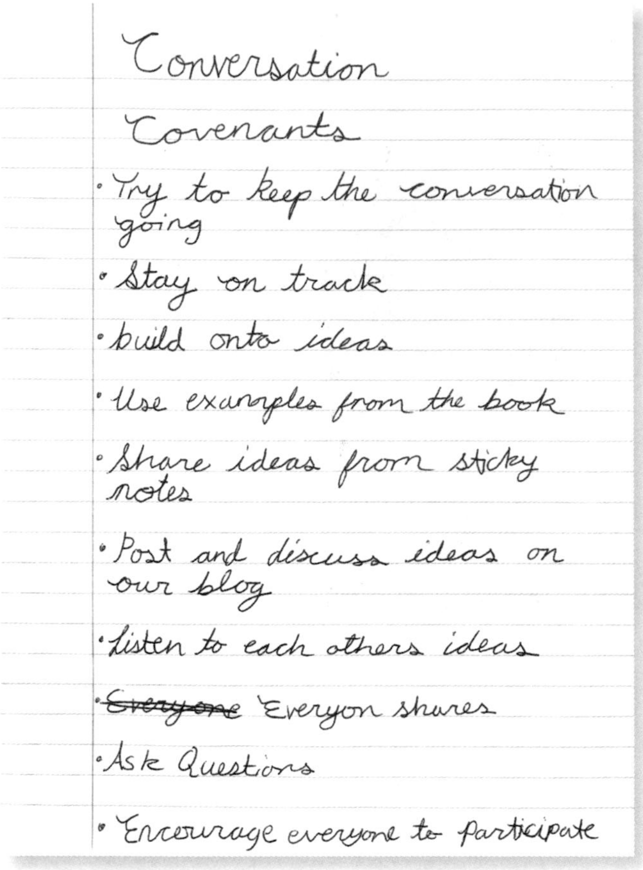

Conversation Covenants

- Try to keep the conversation going
- Stay on track
- build onto ideas
- Use examples from the book
- Share ideas from sticky notes
- Post and discuss ideas on our blog
- Listen to each others ideas
- ~~Everyone~~ Everyon shares
- Ask Questions
- Encourage everyone to participate

Figure 4.1 Ahmad's Club Conversation Covenants

No imposed sentence starters. No limits on ways of responding. Although roles, rules, and sentence starters may be helpful to some teachers and students when working in book clubs, it is our experience that books clubs operating within imposed structures begin to feel stagnant and peter out quickly. This is not to say we should simply stand by and let things run amok! Instead, we can ask students to set their own goals for book club discussions. In Figure 4.1, you can see seventh-grader Ahmad's notebook, which lists the "conversation covenants" he and his peers are striving to meet in their book club. We can look to our students' goals around book club discussions and adjust our own expectations for them.

It's important to set and adjust our priorities based on student goals while keeping in mind three overarching book club goals. If we keep student goals and these three overarching goals in mind as we observe students in books clubs, the information we gather will help us decide how best to proceed. We can create whole-class minilessons or coach individual clubs that provide our students with the tools they need to meet these goals:

Goal #1: Improvement over Time
We admit that the initial book club discussions can be scary. You may feel like throwing your hands in the air and giving up. We know this feeling. However, your goal is to help students have discussions that will improve over time. Consider: Are students deciding what to talk about? Are many voices heard during the conversation? Are students able to sustain a conversation from one or two minutes to ten to fifteen minutes?

Goal #2: Application of Reading Skills
Hearing students talk about an author's craft, character development, and inferences during their book clubs is our dream scenario. We want our students to talk about texts in more sophisticated ways, and we know that book clubs

give them the opportunity to practice their skills. To observe our students transfer the strategies they've learned, we need to teach them practical tools for applying them in their conversations. Consider: Are discussions moving from retellings to more analytical, substantive conversations, and are students selecting strong text references/evidence to support their ideas? Are students tapping into a variety of ways to talk about their reading by identifying and unpacking literary tools such as characterization, setting, symbolism, figurative language, narration, perspective, and theme? Are students occasionally asking questions that include literal comprehension wonderings that can be answered by looking back at the text, but also asking questions that extend beyond literal to critical comprehension that demonstrate insight, critique, and interpretations about the world?

Goal #3: Development of Reading Identities

Book clubs allow students to take risks and to feel part of a reading community. We can help nurture positive reading experiences by empowering our students to talk about their ideas. Many students feel strong as readers because they step out of their comfort zone and work together with a team of readers to dig deep into a text. For many students, the conversations they have with peers in book clubs result in dramatic transformations in their attitudes about reading. For example, eighth-grader Sam explains, "Because when you read in small groups, you can talk about all the bad, confusing, scary, and juicy moments with them!" Consider: Are students coming to know themselves as readers (favorite authors, genres, topics, issues)? Are students more willing to take reading risks such as reading new genres, reading longer texts, discussing challenging ideas, and so on? In what ways do students seem to be growing and changing as readers?

Providing Three Tools for Talk

We've asked ourselves, what does our dream book club conversation entail? What are our students talking about? We admit that when we first asked ourselves these questions, we were shocked to discover that we weren't quite sure what we were looking for. So we challenged ourselves to make a list of everything we wanted to see in our students' discussions. The list looked like this:

* Asking good questions

* Challenging each other's thinking

* Finding themes and symbols

* Talking about the author's craft and purpose

* Sharing their thoughts

* Digging deeper and having an extended discussion about one
  topic

* Analyzing characters and their development

* Talking about their favorite parts and the moments that
  intrigued them

* Reading passages together

* Identifying multiple perspectives and determining rationales
  for different worldviews

* Monitoring for meaning—grappling with difficult ideas

* Critiquing the issues raised, author's craft, character's decisions

* Making connections to people, places, and events

* Relating issues and experiences in a text to their own lives

* Citing strong text evidence to support ideas

When we completed our list, we stood back and gazed at it. Our hearts pounded, as we both stood quietly taking it all in. After a few minutes of standing in silence, we shook our heads. We had set the bar so sky-high for our students' discussions, it's no wonder that we often felt like their conversations fell short of our expectations. Chances are a book club could never meet all of these expectations in any single discussion. Furthermore, we discovered that many criteria on our list were concepts and skills we had never actually taught. And yet, we were somehow expecting our students to demonstrate this in their discussions. We realized that we needed to readjust our goals for our students' discussions.

We began by talking about authentic conversations. What are the "discussion moves" that are made when conversations are working well in clubs? The transcript on page 83 of a book club in Sonja's sixth-grade classroom helped to inform our analyses.

As we examined this exchange between the members of The Bookworms, we thought about the moves that support conversations about texts. We noted that the group of students began by talking about everyone's initial thoughts. They seemed to be using a "What's on everyone's mind? What are your gut reactions to the text?" approach to get the conversation going. As members of the club shared their thoughts, other members chimed in and agreed or disagreed. Right from the start, club members were digging deep into the text by thinking about an essential theme, such as difference, and one way authors demonstrate theme—through characters.

Book Club: The Bookworms

Text: **The Crazy Man** by Pamela Porter

Ella: I keep going back to the word *crazy*.

Jason: Yeah, Pamela Porter uses it in the title and so we know right off we should probably be thinking about this a lot.

Ella: I mean, I use this word all the time, right? But what does it mean? What does *crazy* really mean?

Aaron: And should we be using it?

Nina: It's sort of like a stereotype . . .

Aaron: Like when you use it to describe someone who doesn't seem normal to you.

Nikki: Or who's different. It has different meanings, too. Like when we say our friend is so crazy, we take that in a good way, like they're so funny.

Ella: Yeah, but Angus. People don't think Angus is . . . they think he's crazy in a bad way. In a way that is a bad label and people treat him badly.

We realized that in successful book club discussions, good conversations are often sparked by an emotional response to the book, and then as students dive into sections of the book that spoke to them, they begin to ask questions, search for deeper meaning, and discuss the author's intent and craft. As we thought about the moves that students make during successful book club conversations, we saw that these moves are all steeped in reading comprehension skills. Our students were applying their skills without relying upon a list of discussion questions provided by a teacher. Evan, a seventh grader, says it best. "I would rather have our book club discussions than the teacher's comprehension questions." Recognizing that Evan's preference was also that of countless other students and that all students need support to grow as discussants, we created three tools students can use to strengthen their book club discussions.

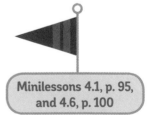

Minilessons 4.1, p. 95,
and 4.6, p. 100

WHAT'S ON YOUR MIND?

The first tool is inspired by a great post we read by Kelly Gallagher one day on Twitter that really stuck with us. He said that his best prompt for students to write about and discuss is, "What's worth talking about?" We wholeheartedly agree. This is the essence of a good book club discussion. This is the key to teaching our students to trust their voices and know that

we value their ideas. If our overarching goal for book clubs is to foster authentic conversations about books, our first goal must be to teach our students ways they can talk about what's on their minds. What do *they* want to talk about?

AUDACIOUS QUESTIONING

Questions unearth deeper layers of thought. They allow us to make connections, pose hypotheses, and search for truth. When students have strong tools for questioning, they are able to dig deeper into a text. We want our students to think of questioning as a tool for developing bold ideas. We want to encourage our students to see their questions as a powerful guide that can lead to richer discussions.

AUTHOR'S MOVES

We want our students to be skillful readers who can do two things—notice author's craft and interpret text through the author's intentional use of literary elements. In our first book, *Teaching Interpretation: Using Text-Based Evidence to Construct Meaning* (2014), we discuss the importance of teaching students strategies to identify and analyze literary elements that support their interpretations of texts. For instance, an author may write the text from multiple perspectives for readers to begin to understand that issues are complex, are angled, and affect people in different ways. Furthermore, an author may include and repeat a symbol. We want readers to notice these kinds of literary elements, ask questions about their purpose, and make interpretations about the larger meaning of the text. During mini-lessons and coaching sessions, it is important to review and teach strategies that help students to accomplish this work throughout book clubs.

Using these three discussion tools can help us focus our attention when we are observing book clubs in action. We can ask ourselves, are we hearing our students talk about what's on their minds, questions, and author's moves? As we listen to their discussions, we can look for artifacts that tell us what's working and what's not, and jot notes about what we're learning on the Observation Checklist (see Figure 3.12). This becomes rich, formative assessment data that we can use to determine the coaching we'll do to support our students in their book clubs. For example, when Dana sat with The Book Ostriches book club, she observed her fifth graders discuss their initial impressions of the main characters of *The City of Ember* by Jeanne DuPrau. As Dana listened to their discussion, she made some quick jots about what her students were thinking about. She noted that they had plenty of personal reactions to the characters, and she was happy that they were sharing their initial impressions and discussing the realism of the characters. However, Dana was noticing that her students were not asking questions. They were missing opportunities to ask why. Why had the author made these choices? Could they be important? As Dana completed her observations of the club, she made notes about the coaching she could do with this club on characterization. She checked to see if other clubs were having similar conversations. If so, Dana could do a whole-class minilesson with some quick strategies for firing up discussions using questions and author's intent. Gathering artifacts and observational notes helps to identify pathways to purposeful teaching. Katherine Bomer (2010) reminds teachers to always notice the "hidden gems" and positive attributes in students' work. To support the work of our students in book clubs, we do our best work when we assess what is going well and what can be improved. This enables us to achieve our goals for students' book club discussions.

Powering Up Talk in Book Clubs Through Written Response

Erica Williams, an English teacher for grades 6–8, expresses a frustration many of us experience about discussions. "Sometimes, I feel frustrated because there's a lack of depth. My students are recapping plot points when they should be deep in analysis, or getting hung up on minor details in the story and not connecting them to anything else. I often wonder if this is something I need to ease up on or let go of." The reality is that it is rare for every book club to have rich discussions every time they meet. We have found that one of the best ways to power up conversations is through writing. Written response helps students reflect on and evaluate their ideas. For example, during the beginning of a book club cycle, students may find it hard to elaborate on ideas; however, encouraging students to brainstorm and jot down their ideas helps them dig deeper in the text, which in turn enhances their discussions. There are several tools we teach students to use.

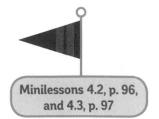

Minilessons 4.2, p. 96, and 4.3, p. 97

STICKY NOTES

There are many different ways we can teach students to use sticky notes:

- Jot down what you're thinking about the text.

- Jot down what strategy you're applying as you read (What are you doing as a reader?)

- Flag key pages as a reminder to cite evidence from the text; ask questions about a character, setting, or plot; make personal connections; make connections to other texts.

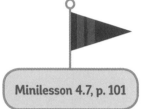

Minilesson 4.7, p. 101

Sixth-grader Jason jotted down the page numbers of a text that correspond with each of his sticky notes and secured them chronologically in his reading notebook. It allowed him to reflect on the development and growth of his discussion ideas over time. In Figure 4.2, you can see a progression of Jason's sticky note thinking over a period of time in his book club.

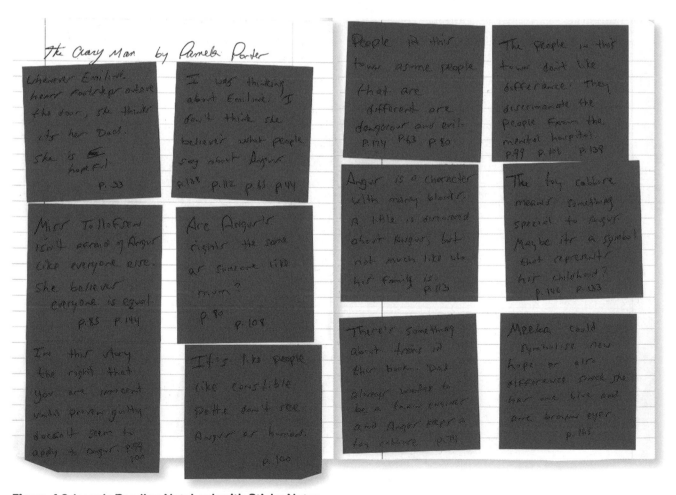

Figure 4.2 Jason's Reading Notebook with Sticky Notes

BLOG ABOUT BOOKS

In blended-learning classrooms, teachers care about using technology in ways that enhance student learning. One of the benefits of using technology in book clubs is that it ensures that all voices are heard. For many students, it is more comfortable for them to express themselves and share their ideas in an online format. Additionally, students are able to link digital texts such as photographs, articles, and video clips that relate to their reading. Blogs can be vibrant, mixed-media spaces that springboard discussions. Club members gain insights into one another that are essential as book clubs bond and form their own identities. This can create a positive energy and excitement in book clubs and act as a catalyst for future in-person conversations. Furthermore, blogs crystallize book club discussions by providing students and teachers with the ability to reflect on a club's progress.

There are several platforms that students can use to blog about their books. Google Docs, Padlet, Kidblog, and Flipgrid are kid-friendly platforms. A simple and easy way to create a blog for book clubs is to create and share a Google Doc with club members. Students can post on the Google Doc and club members can comment. Students can write on the blog before or after the club meets. These types of blogs are great because of their simplicity, especially for teachers who teach younger students or who have limited technology in their classroom. Figure 4.3 shows an example of students using a Google Doc as a blog.

Minilesson 4.4, p. 98

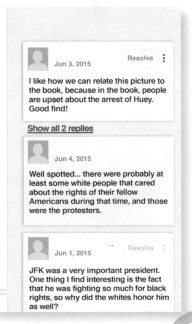

In this photo, the people of Oakland are protesting. There must have been tension in Oakland as well as in the east coast. The picture is also in black and white, which shows that technology wasn't as advanced. The signs say "free huey."

John F. Kennedy
https://www.whitehouse.gov/1600/presidents/johnfkennedy
John F. Kennedy was America's 35'th president and he was determined to make a change in the way blacks were treated. He called for new civil rights legislation and was honored by people of all races. Although he died before the book begins this article makes it evident that he was a very important figure to people both black and white.

Jun 3, 2015   Resolve ⋮
I like how we can relate this picture to the book, because in the book, people are upset about the arrest of Huey. Good find!

Show all 2 replies

Jun 4, 2015
Well spotted... there were probably at least some white people that cared about the rights of their fellow Americans during that time, and those were the protesters.

Jun 1, 2015   Resolve ⋮
JFK was a very important president. One thing I find interesting is the fact that he was fighting so much for black rights, so why did the whites honor him as well?

Figure 4.3 Google Doc Blog

READING NOTEBOOKS

One of our favorite strategies is to give our students a few minutes to write in their reading notebooks before or after their books clubs meet. During this time they might:

- **Look over their sticky notes and jot down what they notice.**

- **Explore an idea they heard during their book club discussion.**

- **Make predictions about their books.**

Pernille Ripp, author of *Passionate Readers*, writes, "We seem to be reflecting kids to death with our requirements to write a little bit about every book they read" (2017, 83). You don't want to take up too much book club meeting time with writing. Instead, the goal is for students' writing to light the spark of conversation within their book club meeting.

MODEL BOOK CLUBS

Book club role models can powerfully influence students in their own clubs. Michelle Kaczmarek, literacy coordinator for grades K–8, notes, "The biggest challenge I have run into in book club discussions can be how I group students. Just because a child is a strong reader does not mean that he or she is necessarily a strong facilitator. Finding that balance in the book club is key. You want members to be able to 'dig' into a text and be able to share their thinking but also be able to get others to share their thinking. And ultimately add onto each other's ideas and possibly leave with a different perspective or point of view. I have had book clubs where children share their thinking but do not connect it to what someone else has said, not allowing for a discussion to happen." Providing our students with access to book club models makes it possible for students to observe strong facilitation skills and discussion techniques in action.

Start by looking for a model book club within your own classroom. Identify a club that can be observed fishbowl style. Ask the role model club to conduct a meeting in the center of the classroom. The rest of the students form an outer circle around this club with their reading notebooks and pencils in hand. For younger students, you might set up chairs around the model club and invite students to sit as they observe. Older students may be able to stand while they observe and make notes. In Figure 4.4, you can see students jotting down the "book club moves" of the model club. The observation period can last anywhere from five to ten minutes depending on the needs of your students. Teachers can encourage students to make note of specific aspects of the discussion:

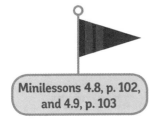

Minilessons 4.8, p. 102, and 4.9, p. 103

- how the group starts a discussion

- ways club members negotiate speaking power

- how club members make use of a text to support their ideas

- how the club gets back on track when the conversation veers off course

- ways club members connect ideas about a text to their lives and the world

- how club members navigate disagreements about ideas

- how clubs wrap up their discussions.

This approach can also be used with just one or two clubs that would benefit, rather than all clubs.

Another way to access a book club role model and use the fishbowl approach is by asking colleagues, particularly those who teach the same grade or one grade above your students, to help you. You and your colleague will need to work out the details. Maybe you can take an "in-school field trip" to observe the model club in another classroom, or maybe it's more feasible for one or two clubs to visit a neighboring classroom at a time.

Figure 4.4 Fifth-Grade Model Book Club

Teachers can also find videos of book clubs online at TeacherTube and YouTube that feature students across grade levels discussing books. You can share these videos on an interactive whiteboard during whole-class instruction time, or ask specific clubs to view them using their laptops or tablets. It is important to select a model book club where students demonstrate how both their written responses and conversation skills contribute to rich discussions about the text. As Sloane, a fourth-grade student, states, "When we're in our book club, we're able to talk about our book on a deeper level."

Balancing Discussions: Loud and Quiet Voices

Minilesson 4.5, p. 99

In addition to teaching students to talk about text with fluency and depth, we'll also need to teach strategies that support how much and how often each student talks. If we were to place the frequency of talk on a continuum, on one side would be the louder voices in our classrooms. We've all had students who dominate partner talk and small-group and whole-class discussions. Their hands are constantly in the air, waving emphatically as if they're ready to rocket out of their seats. On the opposite side of the continuum would be the quieter voices. We're barely able to hear these students even say hello as they enter the classroom, let alone articulate their ideas out loud. Instead, they are comfortable in the background while others battle for center stage. When Kara Pranikoff wrote *Teaching Talk*, we cheered! Finally, we had spot-on strategies at our fingertips to help our students experience a better balance in their discussions. "The depth of ideas is not measured by the speed of their creation," Kara explains, and she teaches us that dialogue is not just about contributing insightful ideas, but about actively listening (2017, 45). Book clubs are opportunities for students to recognize the dynamic relationship that Kara notes between speaking and listening. To help students hone these skills, we've used silence. "Speech is silver and silence is golden." The latter and popular part of this idiom has been used to emphasize that sometimes, silence is better than speech. And sometimes silence is just what's needed to strengthen discussions. This may seem like an oxymoron, but we've found it to be a worthwhile approach for book clubs because it sparks lively silent discussions where the voices of many club members are heard. Additionally, silence can help students develop strong listening skills that benefit conversations. There are two ways you can invite book clubs to engage in a silent discussion.

Minilesson 4.10, p. 104

INSTANT MESSAGING

Club members meet briefly and students grab an index card. Students use their cards to create a quick "What's on Your Mind?" response about the reading. Cards are shuffled and a club member picks one at random. This index card response becomes the prompt that all club members will respond to in their reading notebooks or on a blog. The benefits of doing this on a blog is that students can read, react, and respond to one another, instantly, in real time. Trust us when we say you'll observe students who are highly engaged in this process. They may laugh aloud at the humor of a club member or furrow their brows in disagreement with an idea, but fingers will fly across the keyboard as students virtually jump into the conversation. In Figure 4.5, fifth-graders Sara and Alex engage in instant messaging with club members as they "silently discuss" *Drowned City* by Don Brown. If your students are using reading notebooks, they can write for an allotted time and then pass their notebooks to a fellow club member who will read and respond to their thoughts. This strategy allows all club members, loud and quiet, to participate in the conversation and be heard.

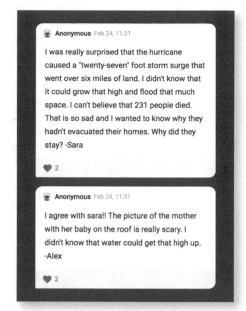

Figure 4.5 Sara's and Alex's Instant Messages About the Graphic Novel *Drowned City*

SILENT CHART CHAT

Provide students with a large piece of paper. Club members select an "audacious question" about their reading. This question is written in the middle of the paper. One at a time, students take turns responding to this question by writing in the available space around the question. Ask students to read each of the written responses before writing theirs and challenge them to provide new insight with their response, rather than repeating what's already there. Members of The Book Ostriches make use of a silent chart chat to discuss a pivotal point in their reading of *The City of Ember* by Jeanne DuPrau. A benefit of this method is that while students are waiting for their turn to respond, they can use the quiet time to read!

We use these silent discussion approaches because they result in maximum participation from book club members. Louder voices pull back as they read the responses of their peers. Quieter voices are present and "heard" as they have a safe way to enter the conversation. Students can use the written responses they produce to spark, guide, and extend future verbal discussions. We've found that using silent discussions as a prelude to verbal discussions, such as in Figure 4.6, is a surefire way to power up talk in book clubs.

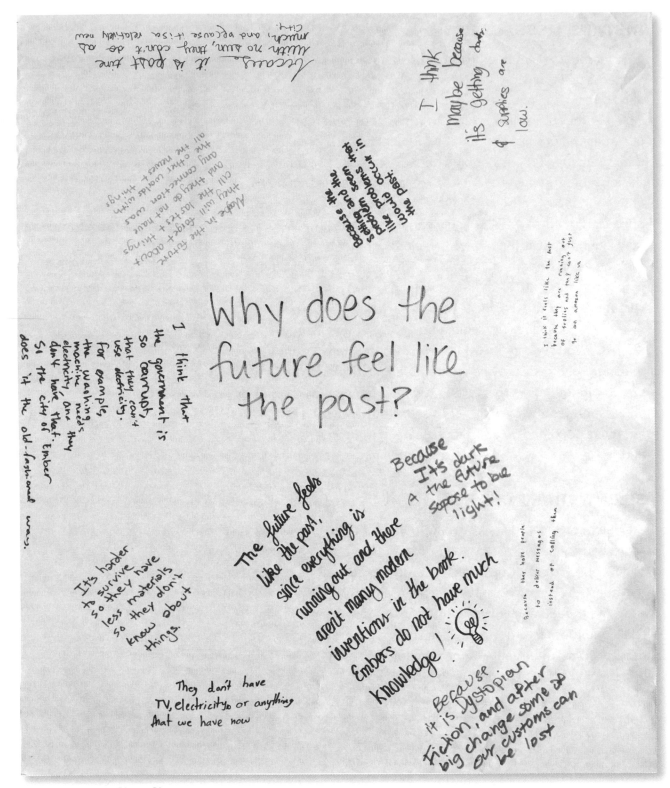

Because it is post time, when no one, they can't do as much, and because it is a relatively new city.

I think maybe because its getting dark & supplies are low.

Maybe in the future they will forget about things all the 105+es+ things and communication was all the movies with oil and other worlds

Because selling food and the problems seem out like it would post.

I think it feels like the past because they are running out of supplies and they can't just go on amazon like us

Why does the future feel like the past?

I think that the government is so corrupt that they can't use electricity. For example, the washing machine needs electricity and they don't have that. So the city of Ember does 'it the old-fashioned ways.

It's harder to survive so they have less materials so they don't know about things.

The future feels like the past, since everything is running out and there aren't many modern inventions in the book. Embers do not have much knowledge!

Because It's dark & the future spose to be light!

Because they have people to deliver messages instead of calling them

They don't have TV, electricityo or anything that we have now

Because it is Dystopian fiction, and after a big change some of our customs can be lost

Figure 4.6 Silent Chart Chat

Breathing New Life into Discussions

"If everything was perfect, you would never learn and you would never grow" [BrainyQuote, n.d.]. Beyoncé Knowles' perspective is one we'll want to adopt as teachers and share with our students as they embark on book club journeys with their peers. When we embrace the imperfect, lean into instead of away from challenges, and recognize that with patience and practice progress is made—we learn. We grow. Part of reexamining and refreshing our practice involves asking ourselves, "How can we reenergize our teaching around book club talk?" We do this by embracing the authentic ways kids talk to each other, and we provide coaching and strategies that empower them to become independent and confident discussants.

Chapter Four Resources at a Glance

IDEAS	SPECIFICS	RESOURCES
Adjust priorities for discussion goals in book clubs! Lean into the authentic ways students communicate.	*How can I honor the ways students talk in their clubs, without letting things run amok?* Work toward three essential goals: • Improvement over time • Application of reading skills • Development of reading identities	**Lesson 4.1: Teaching Three Tools for Talk** p. 95 **Lesson 4.2: Increasing Depth and Breadth** p. 96
Power up talk with writing! Provide coaching around written responses to help students strengthen book club discussions.	*Which strategies help students to enhance their discussions?* Try a variety of strategies to fire up talk: • Sticky notes • Blog about books • Reading notebooks • Model book clubs	**Lesson 4.3: Writing to Get Discussion Flowing!** p. 97 **Lesson 4.4: Reflecting After Book Clubs Meet** p. 98 **Lesson 4.7: Fueling Discussions with Sticky Notes** p. 101
Balance loud and quiet voices! Utilize silence to encourage all members to contribute and listen to each other's ideas.	*How do I get students to avoid dominating discussions without squashing their enthusiasm and help quieter voices feel comfortable sharing?* Invite clubs to engage in a silent discussion using methods such as: • Instant messaging • Silent chart chat	**Lesson 4.5: Creating Spaces for Loud and Quiet Voices** p. 99 **Lesson 4.10: Strengthening Listening Skills** p. 104
Encourage students to reflect on their book club discussions! Invite students to reflect on what's working well and to identify areas that are in need of fine-tuning.	*How do I help students escape the discussion rut they've gotten into?* Provide coaching in the following areas: • Varying talk topics • Monitoring off-task talk • Meaningful and powerful ways to end discussions	**Lesson 4.6: What Should We Talk About Now?** p. 100 **Lesson 4.8: Nudging Our Way Back into the Conversation** p. 102 **Lesson 4.9: Drawing Discussions to a Close** p. 103

PATHWAY MINILESSONS

Teaching Three Tools for Talk

4.1

Pitfall: It can be difficult for some clubs to get the conversation going. They may have a hard time generating an idea to talk about. Or perhaps they have lots of ideas but are having trouble figuring out how to start.

Pathway: Try one of our *three* tried-and-true strategies for helping clubs get their conversations started (see Figure 4.7):

1) **What's on Your Mind?** This strategy teaches club members to trust their voice. And this strategy lets them know that their ideas are valuable. Invite club members to write an idea on a sticky note that they believe might have "long legs" to stretch a conversation across a span of time. Club members can review each other's sticky notes and select one to get started. If the conversation wanes, they can move on to another sticky note idea.

2) **Audacious Questioning.** Questioning is innate to young children, who as truth seekers are always looking for ways to understand the world. This strategy invites book club members to tap into this power to develop bold ideas. Club members may begin their meeting by making a collective list of questions. This often leads to even more questions! After a few minutes, club members select one question to discuss and delve deeper into their reading.

3) **Author's Moves.** When students learn how to read like a writer, they are studying the craft moves of an author. Club members can get a discussion going by paying attention to the author's craft. For example, students can unpack literary elements of a text. They can make a list of possible symbols in a text and revisit key passages to determine what each symbol might represent. Or, if students are reading nonfiction, they might discuss how authors use particular structures to convey meaning.

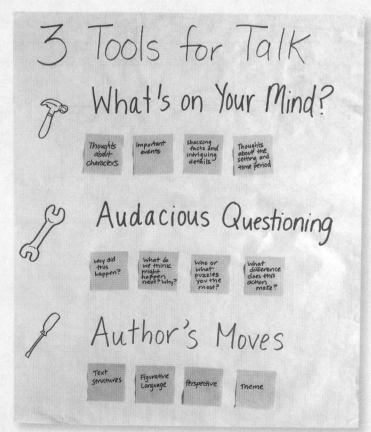

Figure 4.7 Three Tools for Talk Chart

4.2

Increasing Depth and Breadth

Pitfall: Club discussions consist mostly of retellings or summaries of what members read. Club members are experiencing difficulties having discussions that demonstrate greater depth about their reading.

Pathway: Display a chart that reviews the literary elements (see Figure 4.8a) and key questions readers think about related to each element. For example, the chart might include the following:

Perspective—To understand the particular point of view in a text, ask yourself: "Through whose eyes am I seeing the events of the story? Whose voice is being used to tell me about what I'm reading? In what ways is this helpful? In what ways might I be missing something?"

For clubs that are striving to move beyond summarizing, encourage students to keep track of how literary elements factor into their conversations. Figure 4.8b shows how one club worked together on a Google Doc to reference specific literary elements as they read. They color-coded their responses to signal each member's ideas. They also used the guiding questions about the literary element on the class chart and applied them to their reading as they discussed. Each day the club met, they consulted their Google Doc to help them dig deeper and have more analytical conversations.

Jenice Mateo-Toledo, an English language learner specialist, reminds us that it is important for many students to begin a discussion by summarizing. This helps students to make sure that they've comprehended the reading and provides an opportunity to repair meaning when needed. Once literal comprehension is in check, students can move toward discussions that involve inferential and critical thinking.

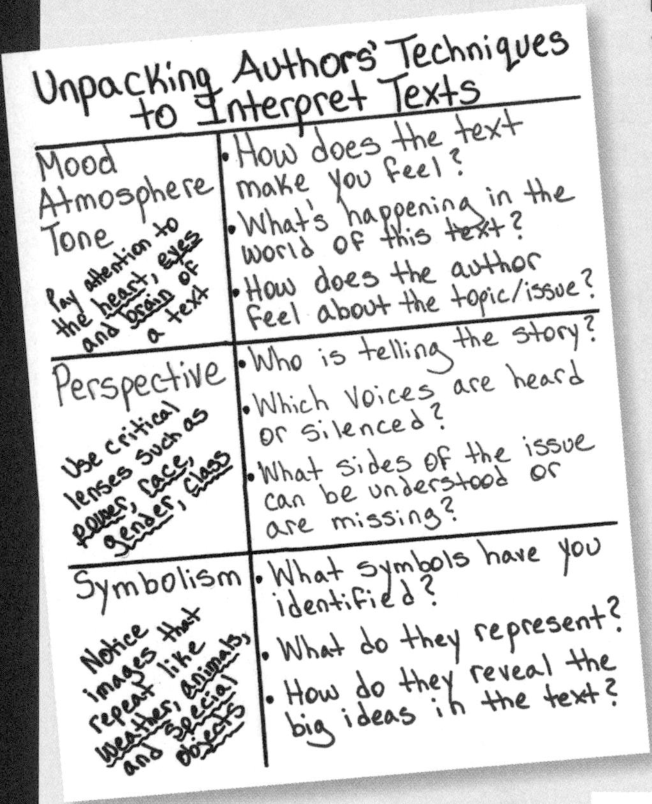

Unpacking Authors' Techniques to Interpret Texts

Mood Atmosphere Tone Pay attention to the heart, eyes and brain of a text	• How does the text make you feel? • What's happening in the world of this text? • How does the author feel about the topic/issue?
Perspective Use critical lenses such as power, race, gender, class	• Who is telling the story? • Which voices are heard or silenced? • What sides of the issue can be understood or are missing?
Symbolism Notice that images that repeat like weather, animals and special objects	• What symbols have you identified? • What do they represent? • How do they reveal the big ideas in the text?

Figure 4.8a (above)
Literary Elements Chart

Figure 4.8b (right)
Literary Elements Google Doc

Track the Literary Elements as You Read

Be sure to check your reading notebook for notes about the literary elements.

Text: *The City of Ember*
Author: Jeanne DuPrau

Literary Elements	Connections to Reading
Mood, Tone, Atmosphere	scary dreary dark depressing
Perspectives	Lina- worried about Poppy, her grandmother, more concerned about family than the city, very sensitive Doon- very worried about the city falling apart, wants to be an electrician so he can be the hero who saves everyone, very serious Granny- very confused, knows there is a big secret but can't remember it Mrs. Murdow- Is a believer, thinks the "Builders" will return to save them
Symbolism	Colored pencils- symbolize the world and brights colors that was lost, Lina's love of art, Lina's fake city Lina's Messenger Cape- shows the importance of her job Box- locked, lost, symbolizes hope

Writing to Get Discussion Flowing!

4.3

Pitfall: Club members are able to start a conversation, but it fizzles quickly. Ideas are sparse and difficult to build upon.

Pathway: Discuss the power of written responses, particularly during silent discussions, as a way to power up talk in book clubs. To help students linger over a discussion idea, ask students to select one topic they'd like to discuss during their meeting. Then, encourage students to marinate in this idea independently and silently by engaging in a "focus write." Similar to a "free write," the goal is for students to fill their reading notebook page or blog wall with as many thoughts and ideas as they can about the topic they've selected for five minutes. In Figure 4.9, a club member takes a few minutes prior to his club meeting to think through his ideas about *Holes* by Louis Sachar. You may suggest that the club use a timer. When the timer goes off, it's time for students to use their writing to engage in a sustained conversation!

Our special education colleagues recommend that club members select a discussion topic the day before the meeting. This gives students an opportunity to have more time to develop their ideas in writing in the resource room and/or after school as well receive support from a peer or their teacher if needed.

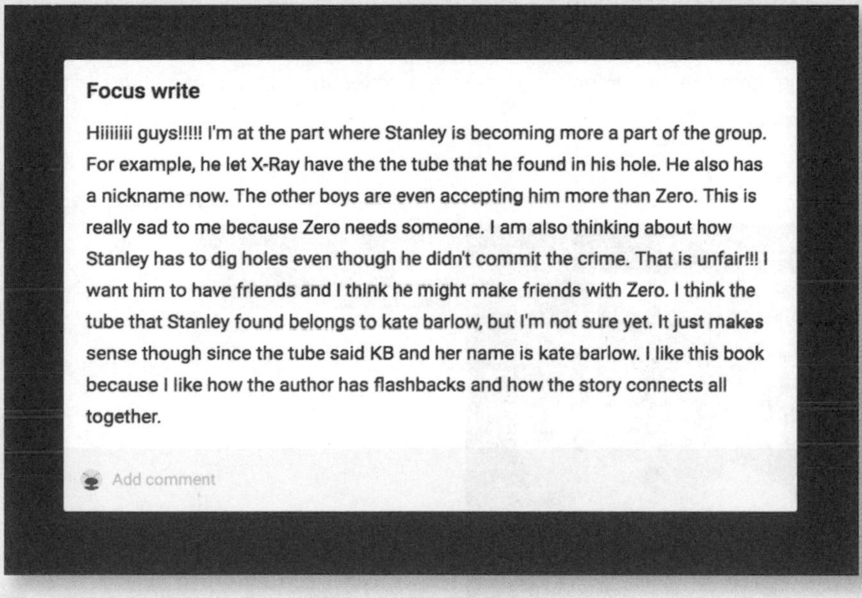

Focus write

Hiiiiiii guys!!!!! I'm at the part where Stanley is becoming more a part of the group. For example, he let X-Ray have the the tube that he found in his hole. He also has a nickname now. The other boys are even accepting him more than Zero. This is really sad to me because Zero needs someone. I am also thinking about how Stanley has to dig holes even though he didn't commit the crime. That is unfair!!! I want him to have friends and I think he might make friends with Zero. I think the tube that Stanley found belongs to kate barlow, but I'm not sure yet. It just makes sense though since the tube said KB and her name is kate barlow. I like this book because I like how the author has flashbacks and how the story connects all together.

Add comment

Figure 4.9 Student's Focus Write Using Padlet

4.4

Reflecting After Book Clubs Meet

Pitfall: Rather than approach discussions as a continuous dialogue among peers, clubs treat each discussion as a stand-alone experience.

Pathway: For discussions to truly thrive in book clubs, members must reflect on the ideas of their peers. These ideas will at times challenge them and at other times be in alignment with their thinking. And sometimes, discussions will leave them puzzled. To help students think about their club discussions and to approach future discussions by arcing back to previous ones, invite students to write a reflection at the end of their club meetings. These reflections can be done on a blog, in students' reading notebooks, or on a platform like Flipgrid. In Figure 4.10, you can see a student who used Flipgrid to reflect. Her peers also recorded their reflections, and all members of the club accessed these and responded prior to their next meeting.

The reflection prompt should be simple and open-ended to allow several entry points for students. For example:

> What struck you or will stay with you as a result of your club discussion today?
> In what ways did your participation today contribute toward the achievement of your club's goals?

Prior to the next club meeting, students should read or view their reflections to prepare for the upcoming conversation. This practice of reflection can become a part of the routine planning of book clubs.

Figure 4.10 Student's Flipgrid Reflection Blog

Creating Spaces for Loud and Quiet Voices

Pitfall: Some club members seem to be dominating the discussion each time clubs meet, while others seem to fade into the background and barely speak.

Pathway: Help clubs build a better balance of voices during their discussions. Invite club members to be part of the problem-solving so that they are more invested in the solution. Here are two ideas clubs have come up with to monitor for loud and quiet voices:

1) **Count Three Before Me**—This strategy is for louder voices in book clubs. The title essentially says it all. The louder voice pulls back and waits for three club members to speak before he or she does. This strategy encourages the louder voice to also be a stronger listener.

2) **Lean In**—Paying attention to and being able to read body language is an important life skill that can be cultivated in book clubs. For quieter voices, it can be challenging to get into the conversation without the formal, turn-taking structure of raising hands. Quieter voices can signal to their club members their intention to speak by leaning forward. In this way, they have a safe way to enter the discussion when their peers learn to recognize this subtle signal.

For many students who grapple with pulling back or speaking up, it can be helpful to use a reading notebook. For example, prior to the meeting, quieter voices can write down ideas they have for club discussions. They may need to read their ideas verbatim, at first, until they feel more confident about speaking. Louder voices who are trying to pull back can sketch visual representations of what they're hearing from their peers while they're waiting to speak. An example of this was created by a fifth-grade student in Figure 4.11 during a discussion of *The City of Ember* by Jeanne DuPrau.

Figure 4.11 Student's Sketch While Listening to Peers

4.6

What Should We Talk About Now?

Pitfall: Club members are stuck in a rut and seem to be having the same type of conversation again and again.

Pathway: Invite students to shake up their club meeting one day by getting crafty! Ask each student to create a What Should We Talk About Now? bookmark that reminds them of all of the ways they've learned to talk about a text. Give students precut construction paper in a bookmark size, colored pencils, and markers. Students can use classroom resources, including their club members, to decide what content they'll include on their bookmarks. Remind students to use classroom anchor charts and notes in their reading notebooks to guide their work. Once the bookmarks are created, club members will have reminders at hand of all the ways they can unpack and discuss a text. Figure 4.12 shows a third-grade student's bookmark.

These bookmarks are great because they serve a dual purpose. They help students vary their discussions, and they serve as informal assessments for teachers who can see what students have learned during reading instruction.

Figure 4.12 What Should We Talk About Now? Bookmark

Fueling Discussions with Sticky Notes

Pitfall: The sticky notes students bring to the club lack the substance to sustain a discussion.

Pathway: We've reminded educators that book clubs are not the time to require students to write lengthy responses to texts. But if students' short bursts of writing are void of substance, remind students about the use of conjunctions such as *because, so, and, but,* and so on. These help students to name causes, state reasons, show results, and explain purpose.

Invite students to use one conjunction in their writing on each of their sticky notes to help them to elaborate upon an idea and provide greater insight to their thinking. For example, in Figure 4.13, you can see a student's sparse sticky note that says, "Bud's not safe!" This student used a conjunction (*so*) to extend her thinking and provide more substance. The second sticky note says, "Bud's not safe, so he goes out on the road again in order to survive."

The use of conjunctions enables students to connect ideas and thoughts, which can even help them to reveal important themes in their texts.

It is helpful for all learners if they can access a chart or handout that reminds them of conjunctions and their usage.

Figure 4.13 Student's Sticky Notes

4.8

Nudging Our Way Back into the Conversation

Pitfall: Club members easily get off task during book club discussions, rather than applying strategies taught to develop rich conversations.

Pathway: It's natural for student conversations to run off track from time to time. They're with peers who they enjoy spending time with, and socializing is an important part of school. To help club members monitor their conversation, especially when it is unfocused or off task, teach conversation phrases that help to nudge them back into the conversation. The following phrases can be particularly helpful and can be used by any club member who notices the conversation needs to be redirected:

- We need to move on to . . .
- Why don't we get back to the topic of . . .
- On that note, let's go back to the issue of . . .
- That reminds me of what we started to talk about . . .
- This relates to . . .

Because we believe in the importance of student-run book clubs, we want to empower our students to monitor how much time is on or off task and to employ a strategy that helps their club have powerful discussions about their reading. In Figure 4.14, a Google Classroom Announcement reminds students of these strategies.

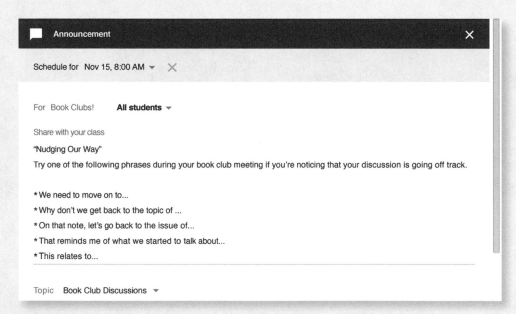

Figure 4.14 **"Nudging Our Way Back into the Conversation" Google Announcement**

Drawing Discussions to a Close

4.9

Pitfall: Discussions seem to abruptly stop when students run out of time. Students need support ending discussions in their club meetings.

Pathway: Anyone who works with children has experienced a student walking away before you've finished speaking, or students' words disappearing in midair at the sound of the bell for lunch or recess. Teach students first and foremost to keep track of time. Also, invite students to try one of the three conversation closers a few minutes before club meetings end:

1) **Roses and Thorns**—This popular activity is done in many families around the dinner table to learn about the positive and challenging parts of each other's day. Invite club members to close their discussion by taking a turn to say one rose (something positive about their book club reading or discussion) and one thorn (something they'd like to improve at their next meeting). In Figure 4.15, you can see a student applying this strategy in her notebook at the end of her club meeting.

2) **Summary**—Although we want our students to move beyond summarizing their reading, that's not to say that summarizing isn't an important skill. In fact, one way to bring a discussion to a close is by inviting one club member to summarize what the group talked about during their meeting. As the student summarizes, the other club members recall their contributions and think about the quality of the club discussion. Club members can take turns summarizing the discussion at the end of club meetings.

3) **Reflection**—We've discussed the importance of reflection in book clubs (see Lesson 4.4). One way students can bring discussions to a close is to write a brief reflection in their reading notebook or blog. What students choose to write about will vary. Some may write about their favorite part of the discussion or reading. Others may reflect on what they're left wondering about, or perhaps something they didn't have time to share during the discussion. Students can use their written reflections to help them during their next club discussion.

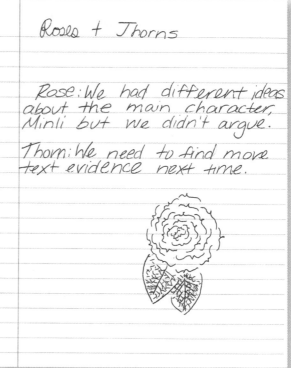

Figure 4.15 Roses and Thorns

4.10

Strengthening Listening Skills

Pitfall: Club members repeat what others have already stated, are nonresponsive, or are defensive toward ideas that are being stated.

Pathway: For students to demonstrate growth as conversationalists, they'll need to be strong listeners. Invite students to try one of the following conversation moves:

- **Repetition**—One way to help students who simply repeat what has already been stated is to ask them to repeat but with a purpose. They begin by giving a short recap of what was previously stated and then contribute their own idea. For example, "Jamie said she thinks that Bud's suitcase could be a symbol. I think that too and maybe the rocks are symbols, but I don't know what they mean." Repeating is a way for students to get into the conversation, and it provides acknowledgment to club members that they were heard.

- **Questioning**—Sometimes when students don't understand or have differing opinions about the ideas of their peers, they disregard them and launch into their own. Teach students to ask probing questions of club members and to work to understand their point of view. Consider displaying a Questions That Clarify chart, such as Figure 4.16, that reminds students to ask questions. Asking probing questions helps to clarify and also promotes critical thinking.

- **Keep the Peace**—We want to encourage students to challenge assumptions and to disagree during discussions to spotlight perspectives that may not have been considered. However, remind students that the goal of club discussions is not to win an argument. Strong listeners may challenge assumptions and disagree, but they do so in ways that make students feel safe and supported. Their book club is a space where issues and opinions can be discussed openly. One way to accomplish this is by providing positive feedback. Remind students of the power of genuine compliments without the use of *but*. Balancing compliments (not necessarily agreements) is one way to avoid confrontations and keep the peace.

Questions that Clarify:

- "Can you say more about that?"

- "I'm not sure what you mean. Can you explain?"

- "Is there a part in the text that makes you think this?"

- "Let me make sure I understand. What you are saying is...?"

Figure 4.16 Questions That Clarify Chart

5: Journeying Through Texts with Peers

Book clubs provide a strong scaffold for readers as they journey together through a text. As our students embark on this journey, we want to be sure that we're providing them with the tools they need to be successful. We want to make sure that our instructional decisions help our students along their path. When students are in book clubs, this becomes a prime opportunity for us to reinforce strategies taught. For example, we can reinforce fiction-reading strategies such as noticing what contributes to character development and identifying the conflict and resolution. We can also remind students to apply nonfiction strategies that help them to identify text structures and determine facts versus opinions. Book clubs allow students to apply the strategies they have already learned and learn new strategies alongside their peers. This requires our instruction to be individualized, specific, and informed by the distinct needs of our students, which enables each book club to thrive.

When we pull back to examine the reading comprehension goals we have for our students in book clubs, we may discover that they are the same goals we have for our students as independent readers. We believe instruction during books clubs should be centered around teaching students to (1) live confidently within a text from the beginning of it to the end and (2) dive deep into a text and construct strong interpretations. The challenge is learning how to make those in-the-moment decisions to address these goals.

Grappling with what to teach and when can be, for many teachers, a terrifying reality about book clubs. But there are a few key steps that can help us make sound instructional decisions. The first step involves listening in on book club discussions and using the Observation Checklist (page 63). We cannot emphasize enough the importance of being a researcher, getting the pulse of each book club, and knowing what our students are *actually* doing. Are they reading with stamina? Are they discussing key ideas? Are they noticing author's craft? Next, we'll want to read students' written responses. Are they mostly summaries? Are they sparse? Do they lack broader connections to larger ideas, other texts, and the world around them? Then, with this research at hand, we can determine which reading skills our students need to learn and what strategies will support their learning. If we're being honest, this requires patience, practice, and tools. We need to give ourselves permission to falter and have faith that we'll become more proficient at using our observation tools as we go forward. And we'll need to trust that our students, undoubtedly with some hiccups along the way, will do the work that's needed.

Although the reading comprehension goals for students may be similar, book clubs are not independent reading. They are small communities where children learn from each other, listen to one another's point of view, and are changed by the reading and powerful discussions they have together. Our reading instruction must be inspired and informed by this. We want to reassure you that reading comprehension *is* happening

in book clubs. You will see and hear it sprouting when you sit in on meetings. You will recognize it blooming when you read their written responses. And as students journey together through texts, applying reading skills and discovering new strategies, you will also notice their reading comprehension strengthen when they draw upon their observations about the world to construct powerful interpretations of texts—as they demonstrate care about the issues that affect their lives and those of so many, as their empathy for others and sense of humanity grows.

Living Confidently Within a Text

It was late February and one of Dana's fifth-grade students, Amy, approached her to talk about her book club reading. Amy was a social butterfly and always had a big smile. However, Dana knew that reading was challenging for Amy. During independent reading time, Amy took frequent trips to the nurse, bathroom, and water fountain. "Ms. Johansen," Amy began, "I finished it in one week! I read the entire book! This is the first book I've ever read in one week." Amy's club was reading *The One and Only Ivan* by Katherine Applegate, and they'd had some dynamic club discussions. Dana had observed Amy taking a leadership role in her club by encouraging her club mates to do dramatic readings of the text, use sticky notes to jot their ideas, and blog about their thoughts. Dana celebrated Amy's victory, for she knew this was the first time Amy had felt confident reading a book on her own. Dana was especially proud of Amy's understanding of the book and the reading strategies she'd used with her book club to fully engage with the text. Amy had experienced the feeling of living inside a text from beginning to end, and she was eager to read a new book with her club.

We want Amy's success for all our students. We want them to thrive and read voraciously together. We want their reading spirits to soar and glow. To help our students achieve this, one of our reading instruction goals is to support our students as they approach a new text and journey with it. What does this look like in the classroom? It looks like a group of students examining their book club book for the first time, saying, "OK, so now that we've read the back cover, let's read the first page and try to figure out who the narrator is." Or it looks like another group of students who are fifty pages deep into their text, saying, "Ah! I think I can predict what will happen to the main character." These moments of successful, joyful discovery by our students are possible with intentional coaching in book clubs that helps them live within the pages of a text.

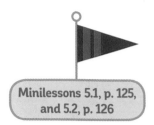

Minilessons 5.1, p. 125,
and 5.2, p. 126

In both fiction and nonfiction book clubs, it is important for our students to work together to live within a text from beginning to end. This requires students to have a strong sense of how stories unfold and help each other along the journey. When Mariana Casanova Keels, a fourth-grade teacher, tried book clubs in her classroom for the first time, she was excited by what she saw unfolding in her classroom.

> My students began working together to take on challenging texts in the safety and comfort of a group setting. I had a group of students reading *Chasing Vermeer,* who were all (through no fault of their own) extremely confused by the beginning of this book (for it does have a rather complex start). Being able to "confess" this to one another, and share in the knowledge that they weren't alone, turned into a great bonding moment and set the tone for the rest of the club. Another group reading *The Name of This Book Is Secret,* by Pseudonymous Bosch, discovered that all its members had at some point tried and abandoned this book prior to this book club. This revelation allowed the students in the group to realize that they weren't alone in abandoning a book and that they now had a "support group" to work through the challenging or less exciting parts. In fact, the experience was so powerful that two of the students in the group decided to become book buddies and start their own book club (and a new friendship!) based on their newly discovered interest in similar books. At the end of the year, one of the students even wrote me a letter to share how much she enjoyed gaining a book club reading buddy.

Such support is also key for online book clubs and when each member of a club is reading a different book. For example, fifth-grade members of The DiCamillo Superfans book club in Figure 5.1 used Padlet as a platform for discussing their ideas about the different books each student was reading.

The camaraderie in this club enabled students to strengthen their understanding of texts and dig deeper into their contents as they revisited and refined their thoughts about texts. As Mariana describes, book clubs allow students to journey through texts together and support each other throughout the reading process.

TRACK THE DETAILS

There is a metaphorical "backpack of reading tools" that we want to give our students as they journey with a text in their book clubs. Introducing these tools begins at the start of book clubs and continues until the com-

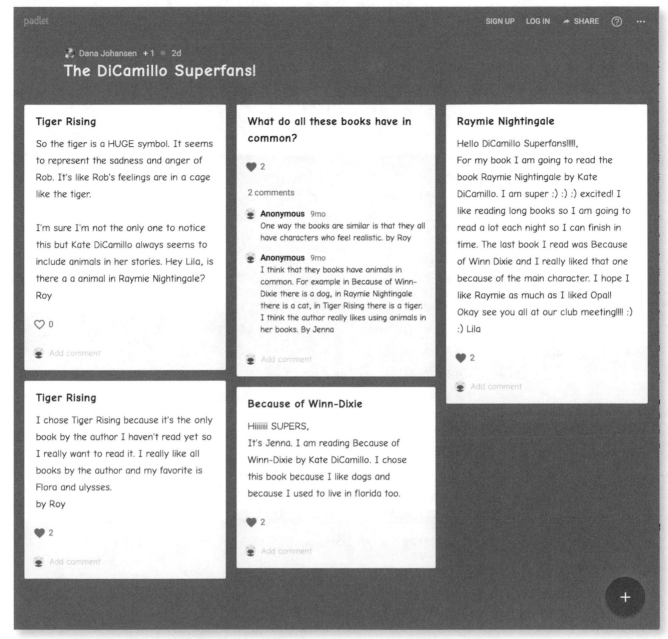

Figure 5.1 DiCamillo Superfans' Blog Posts in Padlet

pletion of the text. These tools are small, quick reminders about the reading comprehension skills our students have learned in class. For instance, at the start of fiction book clubs these reminders might include:

* What do we look for at the beginning of a story? What are you noticing?

* Who is the narrator?

* How will you keep track of the characters?

* What is the central conflict?

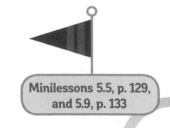

Minilessons 5.5, p. 129, and 5.9, p. 133

109

For nonfiction book clubs, you might remind students to notice:

* How is the text organized?

* What are the text features and how might they help you?

* What is the main idea and what details are supporting it?

* What is fact versus opinion?

One way to help our students track the details in a text is by hanging a chart of these reminders in a central location so all clubs can see it or creating a Google Doc so students can revisit it over and over. In Figure 5.2 is an example of how a whiteboard can be used for teachers and students to co-construct an evolving timeline of the work readers do to track the details of a text from the beginning to the end.

As students journey to the middle and end of a text, these reminders might include:

* What happens by the middle of a text?

* What happens toward the end of a text?

* What is the rising and falling action?

* Is there character development?

* What are the conflicts and resolutions?

For nonfiction, they might be:

* What is the cause or problem?

* Does the author use credible sources?

* What is the effect and solution?

* What seem to be the most compelling data?

* What is the author's main message or call to action?

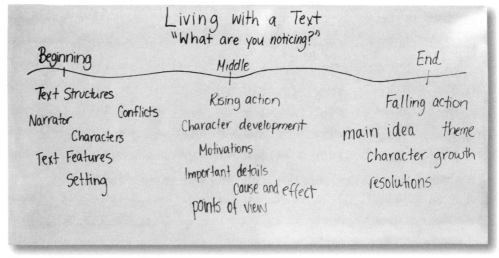

Figure 5.2 Living with a Text

We encourage you to approach your teaching of book clubs the way a coach instructs the team in the midst of a game. Use quick tips and reminders. Remember, you're not introducing a plethora of new reading strategies during book clubs. What does this look like in a whole-class scenario? You might say to your class:

> **In a few minutes we are going to get together in our book clubs. I want to remind everyone to use the class charts in the classroom, especially those about making strong reading plans and having deeper discussions. I've noticed that many of us are in the middle of our book club books, and I wanted to highlight a chart that we used in our last reading unit called What Happens in the Beginning, Middle, and End of Fiction Books? Do you remember when we brainstormed this chart last month? It's a great reference for you to remind yourselves what to anticipate as you journey through your reading together. OK! I look forward to stopping by a few clubs today and hearing your great conversations! Let's get to work!**

These brief reminders help send our readers off to do their work as a club as they live together within a text.

Journeying through texts with peers scaffolds the reading process in ways that benefit students as they develop their skills in book clubs. It enables them to tackle more complex texts in the future as well as dwell confidently within the pages of their independent reading books. Maureen Corbo, a sixth-grade English teacher and leader of her Middle School Mock Newbery Club, reflects on the way book clubs transform the reading lives of her students throughout the school year. She shares, "Although I love seeing the students' enthusiasm as they select the books and discuss them with their peers, I think the true benefit of book clubs is seen later. This year, after we finished a realistic fiction book club and moved into a whole-class novel, I was amazed at the number of connections students made between their book club books and our class read-aloud. The volume of reading during a book club unit gives students not only momentum but also a broader basis for intertextual connections." Students grow together as readers in book clubs, and the support they receive from their peers strengthens their reading skills during the journey as well as in the future.

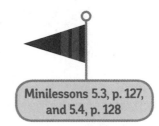

Minilessons 5.3, p. 127, and 5.4, p. 128

Reading with Peers

Since there's so much we need to accomplish with our students each day, reading for book clubs can sometimes be pushed aside and assigned for students to do at home. We like to emphasize the importance of this reading happening in school, as often as possible. Let's not underestimate

the enormous power of providing time for students in book clubs to read together with their peers. When students read together in book clubs, they are able to experience authentic reactions to texts together. This can be the spark for firing up discussions in their clubs. Also, students need time in school to practice reading, which leads to increased stamina, fluency, and reading levels. Furthermore, when book club members read together in class, it provides a window into how the reading is going for our students and the type of coaching teachers can provide to support their goals.

READ ALOUD

We are not suggesting that students read their texts aloud, like the round-robin days of reading instruction, which we know is both ineffective and detrimental for students. Instead, a club member might volunteer to read several pages or a chapter aloud while her club members listen, visualize, sketch, and/or write questions and ideas to discuss later. The next time book clubs meet, a different club member may read aloud. Some students feel more comfortable reading aloud than others, so always let them decide who reads aloud. Another option is to let students read in partnerships within their book clubs. The most important thing is to let the students decide.

CREATE A READING ATMOSPHERE

Many students enjoy creating an atmosphere that promotes reading. For example, some teachers invite students to bring in small pillows to create an atmosphere that feels more like home. Or, for students who love to read on vacation, invite them to bring in beach towels to sit on while they read in book clubs. If all clubs are reading silently, teachers can play ocean wave music lightly in the background to really help students feel like they're reading on the beach!

READER'S THEATRE

For many students, having opportunities to engage in reading in different ways makes reading more fun. As a result, they are motivated to read more. Students may enjoy incorporating reader's theatre as part of their book club readings. Some club members read the dialogue of characters, while another club member is the narrator. Also, students may enjoy acting out an important or favorite scene from their book as they've pictured it in their minds. Of course, it's fun for club members to do this for themselves. But they may also enjoy a small audience of peers, which also serves to pique everyone's interest in the book.

ACCESS TO AUDIOBOOKS

Audiobooks are essential for many students of various learning abilities. As podcasts and audiobooks become increasingly popular, hearing a book read aloud can be an enjoyable experience for all club members and an empowering way for every type of learner to participate in reading. Some platforms and local public libraries provide free access to audiobooks; however, you will want to make sure that you are expanding the literary canon by not limiting students' choices to the classics. To find audiobooks for your classroom, talk with your librarian or media specialist.

Writing Along the Journey

Reading is largely an invisible process. Book clubs help make it visible through discussion and written response. Writing, whether in a digital space or a notebook, helps our students process their ideas about a text and nourish their reading souls. When students share their writing with their club members, they feel heard. They feel that their ideas have been honored. And they learn from each other by listening to new perspectives and opinions.

Writing can take place at different times in book clubs and it can "power up" discussions. Giving students time to write before or after their club meetings is a great way to help students engage in their conversations and reflect about what was discussed (see Chapter 4). We asked Stephanie Seidel, a fourth-grade teacher, about the ways she approaches writing in book clubs. She said, "In past years, I really struggled with having the students respond in a meaningful way to their reading. I always asked them to respond in writing to what they read. This was hard because there were four or five mystery fiction book clubs going on at once, and there was never a 'one-size-fits-all' activity. This year, I really focused on the elements of a mystery story and writing longer about one of their favorite sticky notes, and wow, did I get results! I could really see what they were pondering through their writing and then this in turn was reinforced during their discussions. My students were really excited about talking about books and reading in general." Stephanie reminds us that there is no "one-size-fits-all" approach to written response in book clubs.

One way to assess and determine what to teach during book clubs is to read and assess our students' written responses. For example, we might ask ourselves, "Are students simply retelling plot details? Are responses sparse and lacking text evidence to support ideas?" When we see such straightforward responses this should signal to us that our students are having difficulties.

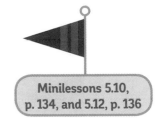

Minilessons 5.10,
p. 134, and 5.12, p. 136

Sonja experienced this with a seventh-grade student. Marcellus was excited to read and discuss *A Long Walk to Water* by Linda Sue Park with his book club, Blue Fire. He was prepared each day with the book and his notebook, eager to share his thinking. Sonja noted on her Observation Checklist that Marcellus seemed to be restating the events he'd read, not only during discussions but also in his reading notebook. Sonja reviewed her observations about this club and noticed that Marcellus was not the only member of his club to struggle to move beyond retelling and summarizing. She used Marcellus' written response to do some coaching in the Blue Fire book club.

Minilesson 5.6, p. 130

I read a recent written response in Marcellus' notebook that made me think that you've been thinking and talking about theme. I think I can see evidence of this when Marcellus writes: "'A step at a time. One problem at a time—just figure out this one problem.' Salva says this to keep hope." I'm so impressed by Marcellus' work. He has identified a strong theme in the story. He also provides strong text evidence. I'm noticing that most of the words in Marcellus' response are quoted from the text. He has an idea about this quote and is off to a good start. In several club members' written responses, I've noticed that the majority of the words are directly quoted from the text. So today, I'd like all club members to find a response like that in your notebook. And I'd like you to elaborate by writing more of your thinking. What is significant about the text evidence you've included? For example, Marcellus can strengthen his work by thinking about what we've learned about theme this year. Theme, we've said, is universal. So Marcellus can demonstrate his understanding of this as he thinks more about hope as a theme in this story and in the world.

Sonja checked in later with the Blue Fire book club and observed the entry in Figure 5.3 in Marcellus' notebook.

Originally, Marcellus' written response work demonstrated that he had been thinking about an essential theme in the text he and his club members were reading and discussing. However, his written work was sparse and mostly consisted of the exact words from the quote he copied into his notebook. His next try includes specific evidence from the text that supports his idea about a theme, but also includes his thoughts about why the theme is significant not only to the story, but in the world. Supporting students' reading comprehension growth during book clubs includes encouraging students to develop their ideas about a text and how it helps them to see the world.

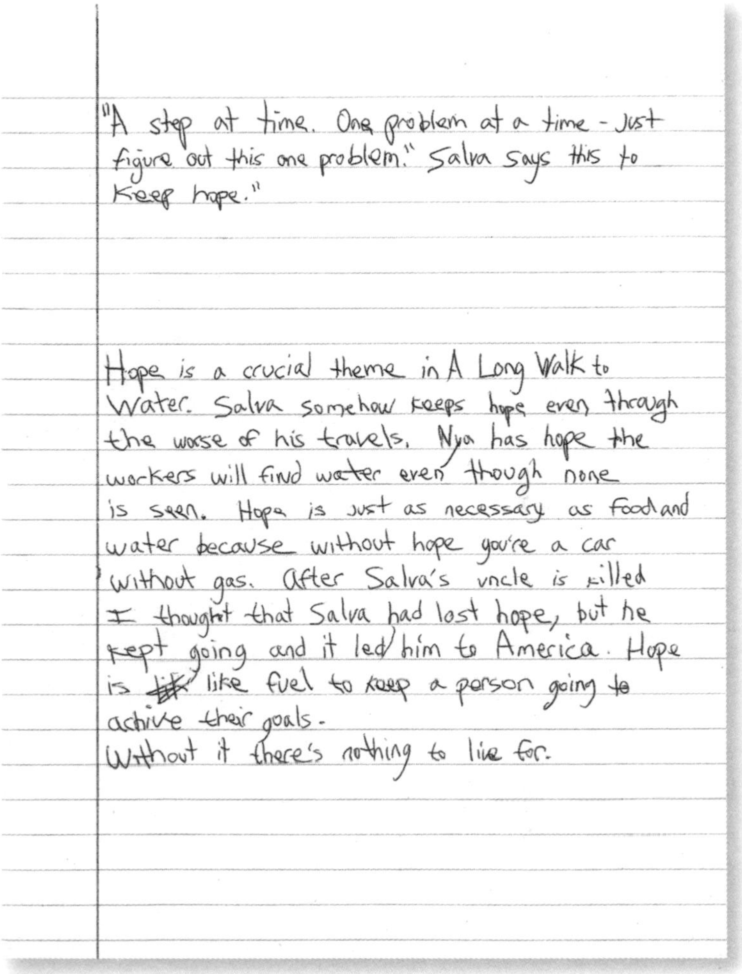

> "A step at time. One problem at a time – Just figure out this one problem." Salva says this to keep hope."
>
> Hope is a crucial theme in A Long Walk to Water. Salva somehow keeps hope even through the worse of his travels. Nya has hope the workers will find water even though none is seen. Hope is just as necessary as food and water because without hope you're a car without gas. After Salva's uncle is killed I thought that Salva had lost hope, but he kept going and it led him to America. Hope is like fuel to keep a person going to achive their goals.
> Without it there's nothing to live for.

Figure 5.3 Marcellus' Notebook Entry

Getting to the Heart of Reading

The world we live in is filled with triumphs and turmoil, and our students carry this with them as they enter their classroom door. News of the latest iPhone, reports of the *Black Panther* movie breaking box office records, and the thrill of seeing a solar eclipse for the first time create a buzz among students that seeps into their book club discussions. The media students consume is also flooded with conflict. Mass shootings, hate crimes, and political clashes are issues students grapple with from day to day. As students dive deep into reading, they bring the realities of their lives and the issues of the world to each text they encounter. Just as divers use scuba equipment for sea exploration, students use their circumstances and experiences to navigate the texts they read and to make interpretations.

Like Jake, a reserved fourth grader who began the year feeling anxious about lockdown drills in his school. Surprisingly, by November, he'd declared his love for them. When his teacher asked why, Jake explained, "'Cause I feel safe when I know that my teachers are thinking about what we need to do if something bad happens here. And even though we have to be silent, we're all together on the carpet and we can read anything we want for a long time with our friends." Later that spring during a discussion of *The Liberation of Gabriel King* by K. L. Going in his book club, Jake felt safe enough to share his worries about school shootings that he felt "are happening almost every day." His peers opened up about their fears too.

Reading brings people together.
Reading provides safety.
Reading calms the storm within our students' lives in
    immeasurable ways.

And Emily, a seventh grader, who shared with her book club that when she was little her favorite books were *I Love You Like Crazy Cakes* by Rose Lewis and *The White Swan Express* by Jean Davies Okimoto, which are about the experience of families adopting children from China. She said, "Because I'm Chinese and adopted, these books meant everything to me. I remember taking out my flashlight and reading *The White Swan Express* late at night while everyone else was asleep. I read it so many times, I knew all of the characters' names and the events by heart. I didn't know why I was so attached to this book then, but I think now that this book helped me to explore my identity." As her book club continued to read and discuss *One for the Murphys* by Lynda Mullaly Hunt, tracking the details that led to Carley being placed in the foster care system, Emily revealed that for a long time, she tried to hide the fact that she was adopted. This led to a poignant discussion about difference.

Reading brings us comfort.
Reading helps us to see and know ourselves.
Reading give us courage.

As students dive deep into texts with their peers, they are both affected by the world around them and inspired to affect the world in positive ways. Book clubs give students the courage to name the world as they see it, the strength to ask why, and the gumption to imagine change when and where it's needed.

READ THE WORD AND THE WORLD

Brazilian scholar Paulo Freire (1970) believed that the world is a socially constructed text to be read and critiqued. The camaraderie that results from being part of a book club enables students to do the brave work of reading and discussing challenging texts, as well as interrogating issues raised within them that are significant to their lives. For example, for Emily, it was important to share with her seventh-grade peers the importance of seeing herself reflected in the books she reads. It was so important to her that she read two particular stories again and again in an attempt to gain a glimpse of herself. But those two texts are not enough. At the International Literacy Association's 2017 conference, Donalyn Miller said, "The absence of a voice is a judgment against it." The invisibility of characters who were like herself made Emily want to hide part of her identity. It also inspired Emily and her comrades to notice how difference seems to really matter in the world and to ask why.

Reading the word and the world is part of the collective struggle students engage in with peers as they journey through texts. To support students in this work, we ask students to keep the following overarching question in mind: What does the text say about the world? The teaching we do in book clubs promotes growth in this area. Figure 5.4 demonstrates a cycle that anchors the work of readers in book clubs as they dig deep into texts and examine the powerful factors that shape their lives.

The coaching involved to help students accomplish this includes teaching students to identify larger sociocultural issues embedded within texts; analyze the strength of a particular stance or position taken regarding these issues; evaluate ideas to make their own judgments; and interpret the author's purpose in writing a text. For example, when The Bookworms club read *The Crazy Man* by Pamela Porter, Sonja observed that club members had frequent discussions about what it means to be "normal." She encouraged club members to track the details of the text that pushed them to think more about this word. Club members engaged in multiple rereadings of several parts of the text and discovered that their initial

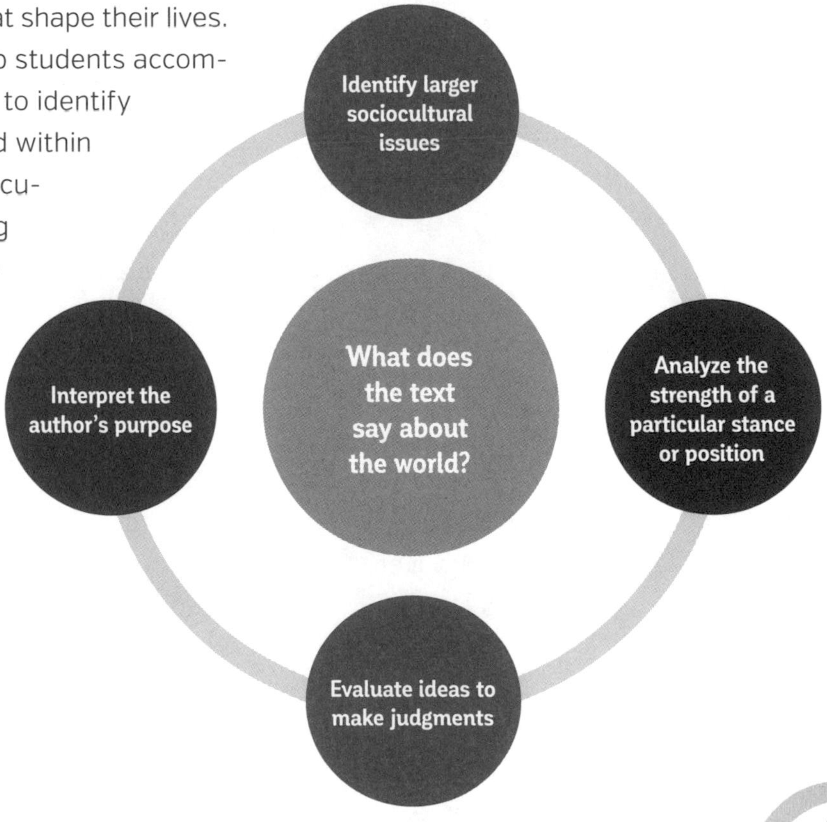

Figure 5.4 Reading the Word and the World

- Identify larger sociocultural issues
- Interpret the author's purpose
- What does the text say about the world?
- Analyze the strength of a particular stance or position
- Evaluate ideas to make judgments

Characters	"normal"	Why?
Emaline	no	- injured foot - Dad left - Angus works on her farm
Angus	no	- he's "the crazy man" - from the mental hospital - talks in 3rd person
Mei Wang	no	- She's Chinese - Lives with entire family
Harry Record	yes	- white - farmer - grows wheat
Mum	no	- no husband - Let's ~~xxxxx~~ Angus live on her farm - grows flax and mustard seed not wheat
Miss Tollofson	yes?	- teacher - lives alone
Jaime	yes	- gets along with people - mean
Joey	no?	- gets into trouble at school
Meeka	no	- One blue eye, one brown eye

Figure 5.5 Aaron's List

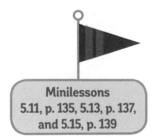

Minilessons
5.11, p. 135, 5.13, p. 137,
and 5.15, p. 139

ideas had just scratched the surface. As they worked to get beyond it, they recognized several issues raised in the text that relate to the concept of what normal is and isn't. Figure 5.5 shows a list of ideas made by Aaron with his peers in his reading notebooks.

Working from this list, students discussed the perspectives of the characters and critiqued them. Throughout this process, students discovered that Pamela Porter uses several craft techniques such as symbolism and parallelism to specifically get readers to think more about the idea of normalcy. This back-and-forth process of reading the word and the world resulted in a sustained critique of issues that students could easily recognize in their lives.

INTERPRET TEXTS AND THE WORLD

In our book *Teaching Interpretation: Using Text-Based Evidence to Construct Meaning* (2014), we wrote about the ways teachers can concretize abstract concepts that benefit readers. The pinnacle of this work is coaching students to identify and support ideas for powerful themes in texts. The coaching we do in book clubs also supports this. During a club meeting, Aaron, from The Bookworms, said, "There's a very narrow definition of what normal is in this book. Maybe this is a theme." Providing coaching that helps students to draw upon the details they've tracked related to literary elements such as setting, multiple perspectives, characterization, figurative language, and symbolism can help students identify and support their ideas for themes in a text. For example, as club members looked across their reading notebooks, they noticed symbols they'd identified and thought about their representations.

In Figure 5.6, Aaron prepared for a previous club meeting by thinking about symbolism. This preparation helped him contribute ideas about theme during the current meeting and construct a powerful interpretation of the text as shown in Figure 5.7.

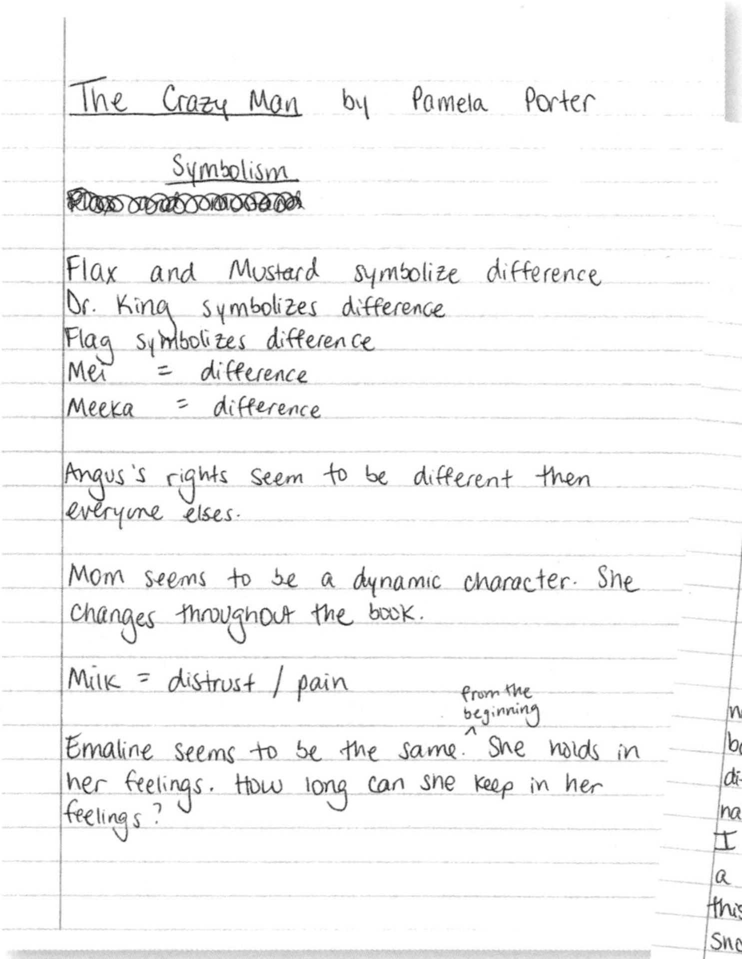

The Crazy Man by Pamela Porter

Symbolism

~~Flax and Mustard~~

Flax and Mustard symbolize difference
Dr. King symbolizes difference
Flag symbolizes difference
Mei = difference
Meeka = difference

Angus's rights seem to be different then everyone elses.

Mom seems to be a dynamic character. She changes throughout the book.

Milk = distrust / pain

Emaline seems to be the same. ^from the beginning She holds in her feelings. How long can she keep in her feelings?

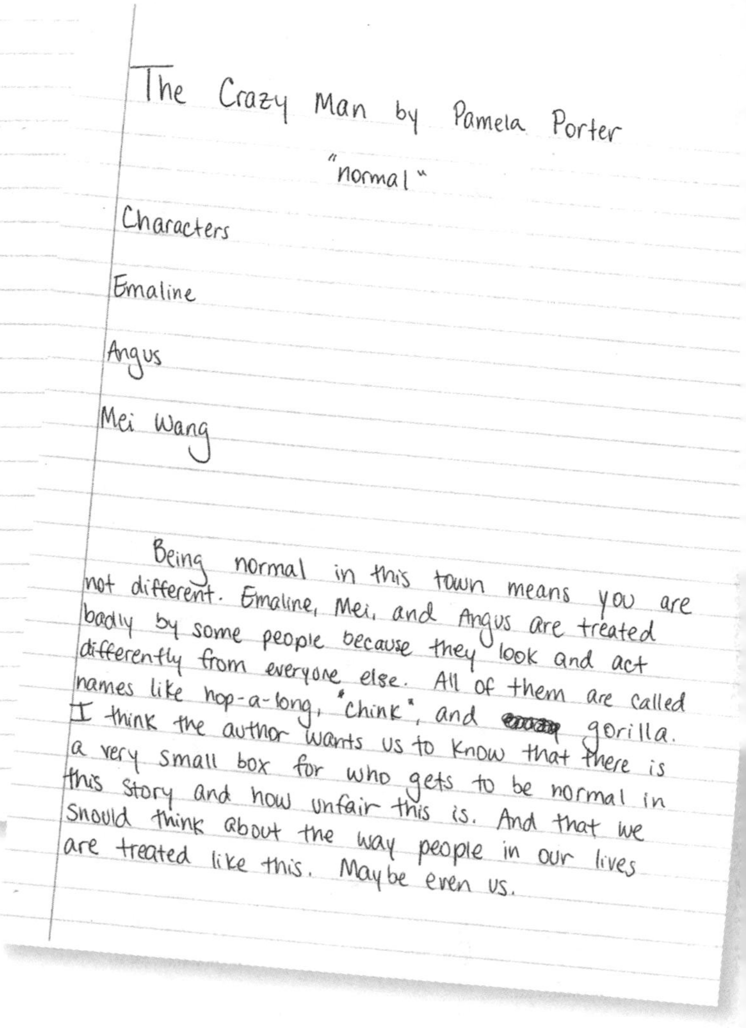

Figure 5.6 (above) Aaron's List of Symbols in *The Crazy Man*

Figure 5.7 (right) Aaron's Theme Paragraph

The Crazy Man by Pamela Porter

"normal"

Characters

Emaline

Angus

Mei Wang

Being normal in this town means you are not different. Emaline, Mei, and Angus are treated badly by some people because they look and act differently from everyone else. All of them are called names like hop-a-long, "chink", and ~~crazy~~ gorilla. I think the author wants us to know that there is a very small box for who gets to be normal in this story and how unfair this is. And that we should think about the way people in our lives are treated like this. Maybe even us.

Coaching book clubs to make strong interpretations of texts involves teaching students to:

1) Revisit their blog/reading notebooks to tap into the emotions a text evokes as they read with peers: What were they feeling throughout the reading?

2) Notice the patterns that exist in the text and also the patterns of their thinking: Which characters/events/ideas did they discuss repeatedly?

3) Identify themes in a text and support ideas with evidence from the beginning, middle, and end: What does this text really seem to be about? What's under the surface?

Such instruction helps brings students closer to thinking deeply about what a text seems to say about the world.

TAKE ACTION

Minilesson 5.8, p. 132

During his 2018 closing keynote address at the TCRWP Summer Writing Institute, author Matt de la Peña said, "Books, especially for children, are a form of activism. What is the job of the writer for the very young? To preserve innocence or to tell the truth? I choose to tell the truth." As students journey through texts with peers, they are looking to see themselves reflected in the worlds within them. And they are digging deep into texts to question and challenge the truths that are revealed. Such recognition of issues and ideas and the bravery to critique them is a powerful form of activism that book clubs foster. Reading changes us. It helps us see ourselves and the world more clearly and perhaps differently than we ever have before.

We want to remind students to reflect on their reading, particularly once they've finished a book together. Two questions that help students think deeply about their reading journeys are: How have you been changed by this reading and the discussions you've had with your peers? How can the ideas within this book change the world? In Figure 5.8, Ella reflects on how she is changed as a result of reading the book *The Crazy Man* and the discussions she's had with her peers and the difference this text makes in the world.

Access to digital tools is another way students can take action by connecting to and with the wider world. Take, for example, the Blue Fire book club. After reflecting on the ways they have been changed by reading *A Long Walk to Water* by Linda Sue Park, club members took several actions.

First, inspired by his extraordinary story and efforts to bring clean water to South Sudan, club members visited the website www .waterforsouthsudan.org to learn more about Salva Dut, whom they had read about in *A Long Walk to Water*. In the process, students applied their nonfiction reading comprehension skills as they read maps, accessed video clips, and learned more about this issue on blogs and in news articles made available on the website.

> What does it mean to be Crazy?
>
> Crazy is a loaded word. It can mean to be mentally ill, or it could just mean to be different, or ~~recently~~ really funny and loud. Because crazy has so many defanitions and interperations, I'm going to be coreful when I use it from now on. Because it can be a serious insult to some and to others they may take it as a compliment. I think this book is important. It helps people to understand that words matter. And there are so many other words to call ~~many~~ people. We should use words with greater core.

Figure 5.8 Ella's Reflection

Also, as students explored the issue of clean water, they kept track of related topics raised in the novel such as the lack of education accessible to girls in South Sudan and other countries in the world. Additionally, students connected information they read to issues in the United States such as the Flint, Michigan, water crisis. Interest in these subtopics led to further reading, researching, and writing. Students wrote feature articles on the issues that emerged from their reading and submitted them to the school newspaper. They also created public service announcements using Windows Movie Maker and WeVideo. To learn how to do this, they accessed resources to make public service announce-

ments made available at readwritethink.org (readwritethink, n.d.). These were posted in Google Classrooms to share with peers.

Finally, students had a burning desire to meet the man whose story galvanized them to take action. Although Salva was not able to visit their school, students and their teachers were lucky enough to arrange a Skype session with him during his visit to New York to attend the United Nations Water meeting. The Blue Fire book club was so thrilled, they asked all of their sixth-grade peers to read the book and arranged to have the Skype session in their middle school auditorium so that all sixth graders could meet Salva.

Because, as Matt de la Peña states, the job of writers is to tell the truth, students are forever changed when they read and journey through texts with peers in book clubs. And the actions they take—from recommending a beloved book to a peer, to informing others about important topics and issues in various ways—are changes that in turn benefit the world.

Breathing New Life into Journeying Through Texts with Peers

In her important and timely book *Being the Change*, Sara Ahmed helps teachers think about the valuable work of social comprehension. She tells teachers, "Our thinking will change often as we practice being more socially literate citizens of the world, so we allow for and model the same for our students as we construct comprehension and cultivate our empathy together" [2018, 25]. This is what we want for our students: to be "socially literate citizens of the world." When students journey through texts together, their experience is influenced not only by their own individual thoughts, but by the perspectives of others. This has the power to shape students' reading identities because they learn how to view a text through multiple lenses. In book clubs, students walk together in each other's shoes.

Chapter Five Resources at a Glance

IDEAS	STRATEGIES	RESOURCES
Teach students to track the details of a text! Encourage students to apply reading comprehension skills they've learned and are learning in their book clubs.	*How do I help students to live confidently within a text from beginning to end?* Co-construct an evolving timeline that demonstrates what readers do to track details in both fiction and nonfiction reading.	**Lesson 5.1: Journeying Through Fiction** p. 125 **Lesson 5.2: Journeying Through Nonfiction** p. 126 **Lesson 5.3: Keeping Track of Characters** p. 127 **Lesson 5.14: Keeping Track of Events** p. 138
Encourage students to read together in book clubs! Reading together strengthens club bonds as students experience challenging, exciting, and thought-provoking parts together while improving stamina, fluency, and expression.	*How can I support students as they read texts together during club meetings?* Invite students to explore new and exciting ways to read together.	**Read Aloud** p. 112 **Create a Reading Atmosphere** p. 112 **Reader's Theatre** p. 112 **Access to Audiobooks** p. 113
Use students' written responses to determine reading strategies to teach! Support students' reading comprehension growth in book clubs by helping them to develop their ideas about texts in their writing.	*Which reading strategies do I teach?* Provide coaching that supports students' work toward: • Elaborating upon ideas • Applying strategies for getting unstuck • Including text references/evidence • Using digital tools to support reading comprehension • Annotating texts • Determining importance • Identifying and analyzing literary elements	**Lesson 5.6: Identifying Essential Themes** p. 130 **Lesson 5.7: Repairing Misunderstandings** p. 131 **Lesson 5.9: Determining What's Important** p. 133 **Lesson 5.10: Annotating to Cozy Up with Texts** p. 134 **Lesson 5.11: Identifying Perspectives** p. 135 **Lesson 5.12: Slowing Down to Take in the Setting** p. 136 **Lesson 5.13: Locating and Analyzing Symbols** p. 137
Encourage students to read the word and the world! Engage club members in the collective struggle of making sense of texts and what they say about the world.	*What is the teaching that helps students to dive deep into texts?* Provide coaching that assists students with: • Identifying larger sociocultural issues within a text • Analyzing a particular stance or position • Evaluating ideas to make judgments • Interpreting the author's purpose • Seeing texts as a form of activism	**Read the Word and the World** p. 117 **Lesson 5.8: Critiquing a Text** p. 132 **Lesson 5.11: Identifying Perspectives** p. 135

PATHWAY MINILESSONS

Journeying Through Fiction

Pitfall: Club members need tools to independently journey through a fiction text. For instance, they may be unsure how the book is set up, who the narrator is, and how a fictional story plot might unfold.

Pathway: Consider creating with students a living chart, such as the one on page 110. The chart should show students the types of details they can look for and the thinking that occurs as they journey through a text from beginning to end.

You can also try giving your book club(s) a fiction book scavenger hunt. This activity usually takes about five minutes, and it helps students preview their text and its features. In Figure 5.9, you can see a scavenger hunt example based on the text *The Lightning Thief* by Rick Riordan.

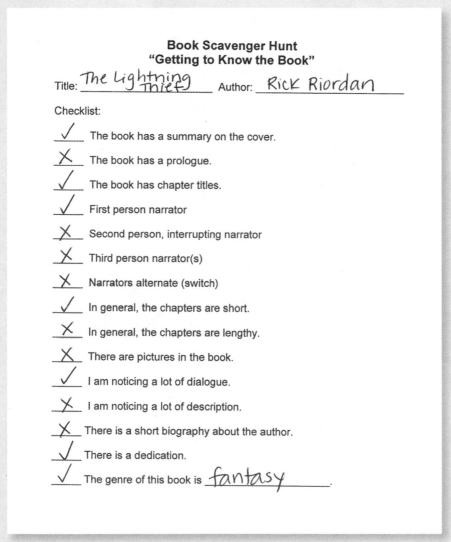

Figure 5.9 Scavenger Hunt

Journeying Through Nonfiction

Pitfall: Club members are having difficulty making use of the structures and features of nonfiction. As a result, they are experiencing challenges with comprehension.

Pathway: Provide club members with a brief article, perhaps from *National Geographic Kids* or *Time for Kids*. Ask club members to work together to annotate the article by identifying the structures and features of nonfiction. Support their work by referring them to a classroom anchor chart or existing resources in their reading notebook. The annotation is not simply a label, but also a brief phrase or sentence. When this is completed, this resource should be handy whenever the club meets so that students can apply this knowledge to the particular nonfiction text they're reading. In Figure 5.10, a student annotates an article.

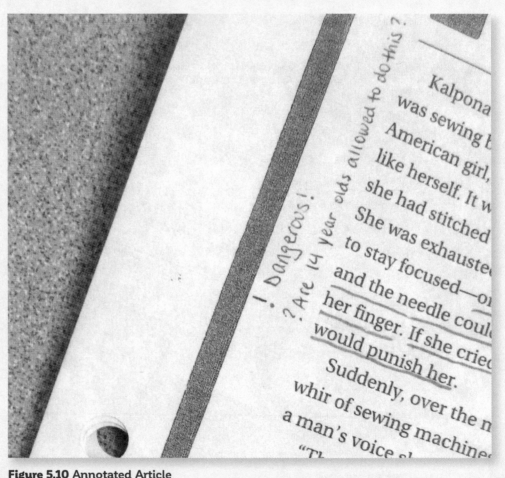

Figure 5.10 Annotated Article

Keeping Track of Characters

Pitfall: Sometimes, club members lose track of the major and minor characters, and they are having difficulty traveling through their text.

Pathway: Our favorite solution is an oldie, but goodie. We recommend that you give your students index cards that will serve as bookmarks, and on these cards have your students record the names of characters as they encounter them in the text. They should also write a few words that describe the character and the character's relationship with other characters.

Additionally, students should put a star next to the names of major characters. For advanced readers, have students note the character's archetype in the story (wise character, villain, bully, foil, etc.). Figure 5.11 shows a student making use of this strategy in the bookmark she created for *Keeper of the Lost Cities* by Shannon Messenger.

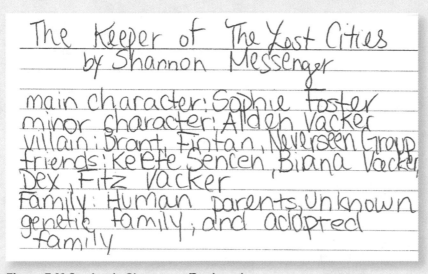

Figure 5.11 Student's Characters Bookmark

5.4 Noticing Dialogue

Pitfall: Students grapple with analyzing dialogue as a literary element in their text. Club members are having difficulty understanding dialogue as more than simply casual conversations between characters.

Pathway: Dialogue can teach readers a great deal about characters and how they interact with others. To help students analyze dialogue, ask them to select one section of their text and with their club members evaluate and discuss its purpose in that particular part of the story. Does the dialogue:

- Reveal a character's personality traits, feelings, or desires?
- Motivate characters to take action?
- Expose a significant detail or secret?

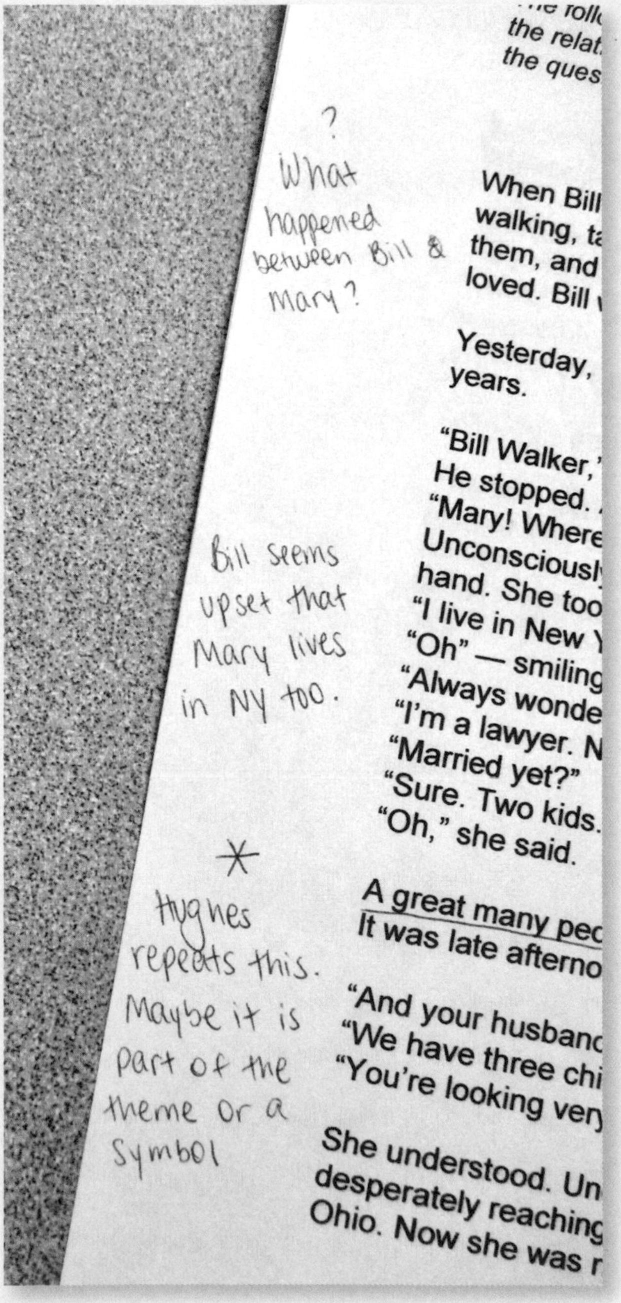

Remind students that the dialogue can serve one or more of these purposes. Their job as readers is to be on the lookout for what the dialogue in their texts teaches them about characters and the ways they act. In Figure 5.12, notice how one student's annotations focus on the role of dialogue in the short story "Early Autumn" by Langston Hughes.

Figure 5.12 Annotated Short Story

?
What happened between Bill & Mary?

Bill seems upset that Mary lives in NY too.

*

Hughes repeats this. Maybe it is part of the theme or a symbol

...e roll...
the relat...
the ques...

When Bill
walking, ta
them, and
loved. Bill w

Yesterday,
years.

"Bill Walker,"
He stopped.
"Mary! Where
Unconscioush
hand. She too
"I live in New Y
"Oh" — smiling
"Always wonde
"I'm a lawyer. N
"Married yet?"
"Sure. Two kids.
"Oh," she said.

A great many pec
It was late afterno

"And your husband
"We have three chi
"You're looking very

She understood. Un
desperately reaching
Ohio. Now she was r

Finding the Main Idea

Pitfall: Club members are having a challenging time identifying the main idea in their nonfiction text.

Pathway: Help students uncover the main idea by discussing the differences between the details in a text and the main idea. First, have students locate details in a paragraph or chapter of the text. After they have identified some details, ask them, "What is the author's big message? How do all these details fit together?" Working with book clubs individually, have students contribute to a chart like the one in Figure 5.13. This will help students practice thinking about the big idea of a section of their text, the details that connect to that idea, and any lingering questions. This strategy is particularly helpful when students are reading shorter nonfiction texts.

Encourage students to practice using this strategy on their own, and revisit the club to see their progress.

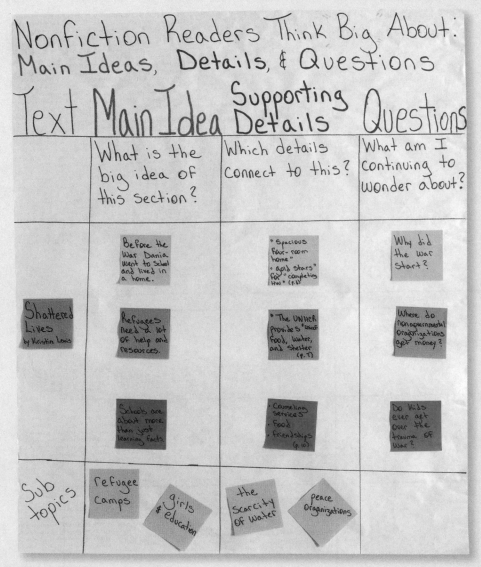

Figure 5.13 Main Idea Chart

5.6

Identifying Essential Themes

Pitfall: Club members are unable to identify essential themes in their reading and support their ideas with strong text evidence.

Pathway: Helping students to identify themes has been a recurring issue in our classrooms. In our book *Teaching Interpretation: Using Text-Based Evidence to Construct Meaning* (2014), we provide ways to make the abstract concept of theme more concrete for students. First, we recommend providing club members with lists of common themes found in literature. This is particularly helpful for learners who may struggle with word retrieval. Next, ask club members to think about the universal message the author seems to be sending readers. To identify possibilities for themes, students should tap into the emotions they experienced as readers and make a list of their ideas.

Finally, to test their ideas and determine whether or not they are in fact essential themes, ask club members to find strong evidence from the beginning, middle, and end of their text. If they are unable to do so, they should cross off the idea from their list of essential themes.

It can be helpful to display a chart like the one in Figure 5.14 that all clubs can manipulate using sticky notes that can be easily removed.

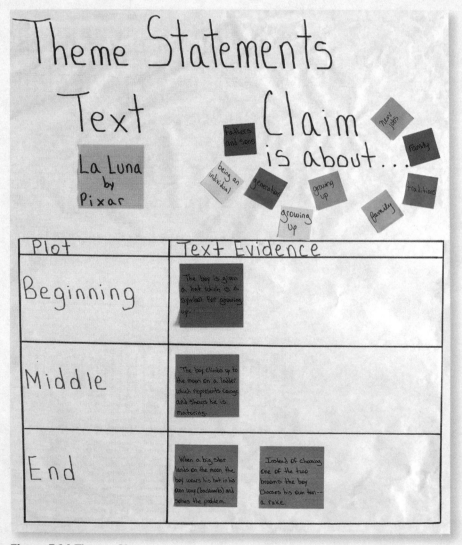

Figure 5.14 Theme Chart

5.7

Repairing Misunderstandings

Pitfall: Occasionally, book clubs have a challenging time keeping up with all that's happening in their text, and they get stuck.

Pathway: Help students implement a strategy for getting unstuck (see Figure 5.15):

1) Stop! Rewind! Go back to the last place where you knew what was happening and work forward with your club's help.

2) Talk! Discuss what has happened in the book so far. Retelling the most important events in the story will move you from confusion to clarity.

3) Reread! Go back to the parts that were confusing and reread them together as a team.

4) Plan! Make a plan for moving forward.

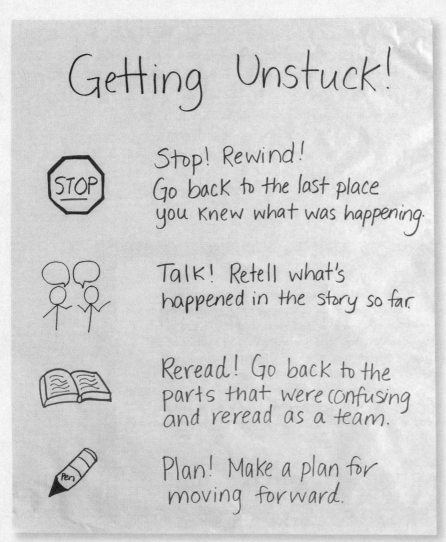

Figure 5.15 Getting Unstuck Chart

5.8

Critiquing a Text

Pitfall: Evaluating a text and forming opinions is challenging for club members. As a result, students miss multiple layers of understanding.

Pathway: Students often attribute a negative connotation to the words *critical* and *critique*. Instead, inform students that critiquing a text is about developing an understanding about its significance. Let students know that using critical thinking skills to evaluate a text is an important part of reading comprehension.

To help students critique fiction texts, ask them to discuss their ideas in response to the question: What is the author trying to say? Provide them with "critical lenses" with which to evaluate a text. Invite students to discuss their reading through the lens of gender, race, class, and so on. In Figure 5.16 a student thinks about *The Crazy Man* by Pamela Porter through the lens of race.

For critiquing articles, essays, and opinion pieces, invite students to first evaluate for their overall impression after reading the text. Then, students can discuss its validity. Ask students to discuss their ideas in response to the question: What is the main argument being presented? Invite students to check for methods an author may have used, which can be used to form a critique of the reading such as:

- generalizing—assuming a specific example will be true everywhere
- discrediting—insulting people's character rather than critiquing their perspective
- assuming consequences—implying a cause-and-effect relationship without proof
- questionable assumption—argument founded on something that may not be true.

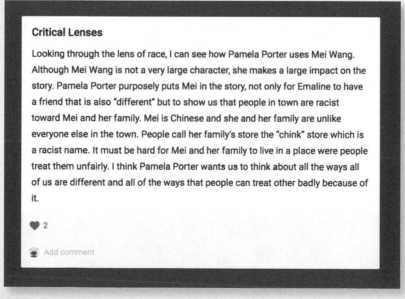

Figure 5.16 Critical Lenses Padlet

Determining What's Important

Pitfall: When reading nonfiction, club members need support to determine what's important versus what's interesting. As a result, students are unable to comprehend more complex texts.

Pathway: Interesting Versus Important is a popular reading strategy to help students determine importance. Although interesting details and important details are not always mutually exclusive, help students determine that interesting details can help to engage readers, while important details can help readers comprehend the main ideas of texts. Have students make a T-chart in their reading notebook or blog like in the one in Figure 5.17. Ask club members to label *Interesting* on one side and *Important* on the other side. Then have club members work together to read a section of their text and list details they find interesting in the designated column and details they believe to be important in the other column. Engage students in a discussion of the following questions about their lists: What purpose do the interesting details serve? What purpose do the important details serve?

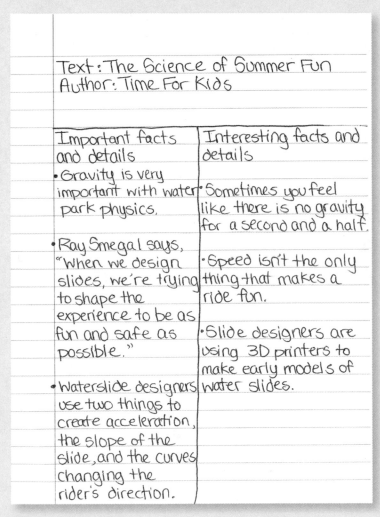

Figure 5.17 Interesting Versus Important Details T-Chart

5.10

Annotating to Cozy Up with Texts

Pitfall: When reading complex texts, club members experience difficulties monitoring their understanding. Texts are read quickly, regardless of whether students truly comprehend what they're reading.

Pathway: Invite students to cozy up with challenging texts by slowing down to focus and engage with the reading. Review the usage of annotation marks to annotate texts when the reading becomes more difficult. Consider displaying an Annotation Marks chart, such as the one in Figure 5.18, for students to access; provide a handout; or remind students to use their notes in their reading notebooks.

Start the annotation process by teaching students to use one or two annotation marks at a time and then add on slowly. When students become proficient using annotation marks, ask them to also write short phrases or sentences that elaborate on the annotation mark. Annotating in this way helps deepen the reader's comprehension, and it helps club members discuss texts in greater depth.

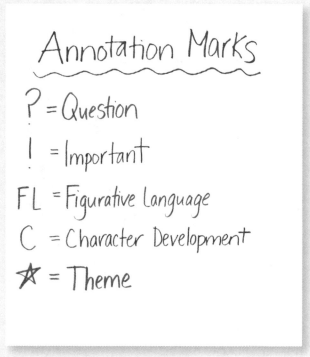

Figure 5.18 Reader's Marks Chart

Identifying Perspectives

Pitfall: Club members need support identifying and keeping track of the various perspectives of characters.

Pathway: One of our favorite strategies for helping students gain insight into the perspectives of characters is also one that brings a great deal of fun to club meetings. Invite club members to play "Hot Seat." One club member volunteers to "become" a character from the reading. The other members write down questions they'd like to ask the character in their reading notebook. Figure 5.19 shows an example of one club member who wrote hot seat questions for the characters in *Divergent* by Veronica Roth. These questions should not simply elicit yes-or-no responses; they should invite thoughtful responses from the club member embodying the character. Then, each student takes turns asking the character a question. The students playing the character use details from the reading as well as their inferencing skills to answer the questions to the best of their ability. If they can't answer, they can pass.

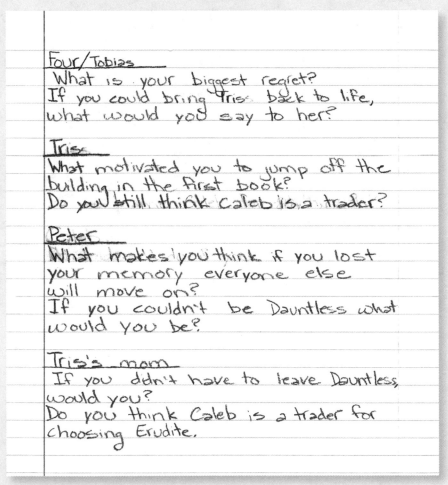

Figure 5.19 Student's Hot Seat Questions for Characters from *Divergent*

5.12

Slowing Down to Take in the Setting

Pitfall: Speeding through the reading has caused club members to miss essential details about the setting.

Pathway: When students miss essential setting details, they miss opportunities to comprehend their reading. Teach students to be tourists as they read and collect "setting souvenirs" that help them to visualize what a place looks like and imagine what it feels like. Students can mark passages where the author helps them take in the setting. In Figure 5.20 a fifth grader visualizes a scene from *Holes* by Louis Sachar and a fourth grader imagines the setting in *The City of Ember* by Jeanne DuPrau. Invite students to reread these passages in club meetings to practice analyzing setting and how it influences the plot and the actions of characters.

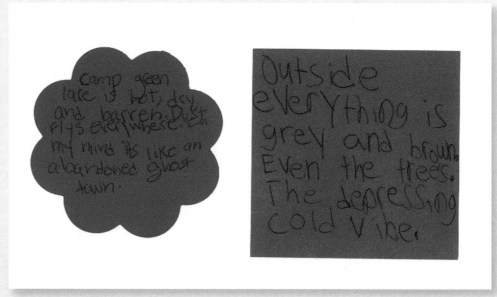

Figure 5.20 "Setting Souvenirs" from *Holes* by Louis Sachar and *The City of Ember* by Jeanne DuPrau

Locating and Analyzing Symbols

Pitfall: Students have learned how to identify symbols in a text, but they are not doing this work independently in book clubs.

Pathway: Review how to identify symbols with your whole class or with individual book clubs. To practice this work, we recommend you use a short text such as a picture book or digital text. The following example uses the digital text "Let It Go" from Disney's *Frozen*.

First, review two strategies for noticing symbols: (1) Look for anything that repeats. (2) Look for any important objects that are meaningful to the character. Have students look out for these as they watch the movie clip "Let It Go." They may find a glove, a crown, a staircase, snowflakes, a cape, and so on. Have students think about these objects. What do these objects symbolize? What might a glove, a cape, a crown, a staircase, and snowflakes symbolize? (Protection, royalty, a climb/journey, uniqueness?) In Figure 5.21, a student uses a graphic organizer to identify the symbols in "Let It Go."

Have your students try this work in their own texts. We recommend starting small by having your students notice important objects and things that repeat. You may add on animals, colors, weather, and more.

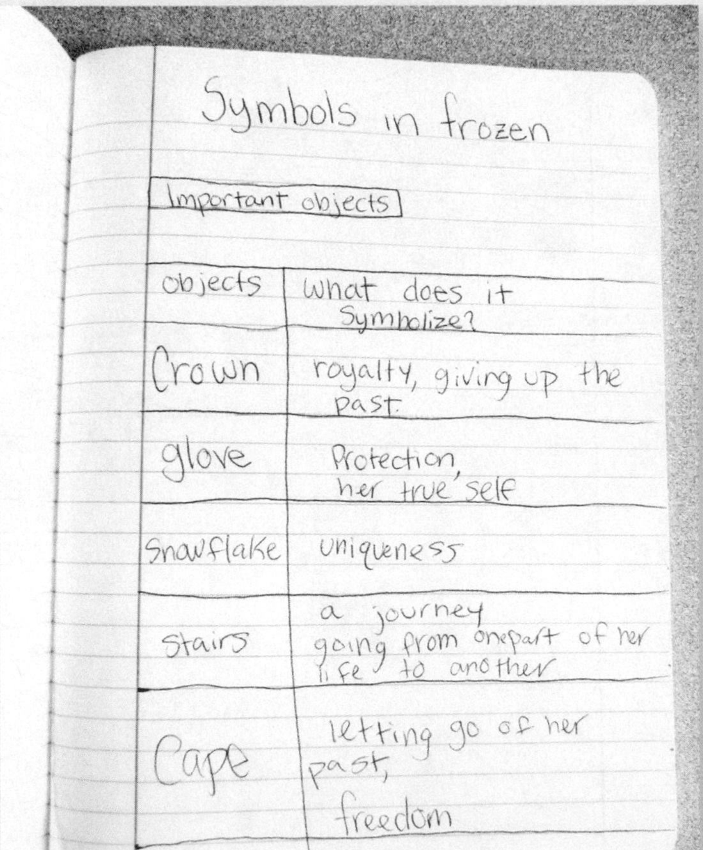

Figure 5.21 *Frozen Student Work Sample*

Keeping Track of Events

Pitfall: Sequencing events can be troublesome for club members. They can become confused about the order of events and their significance.

Pathway: Convene the whole class or individual book club members and talk to them about the importance of keeping track of the events in a story. It is important to delineate how major events in a story contribute to the conflict and resolution.

Have students use sticky notes to flag events as they are reading. Next, have students remove their flags and organize them on a table or the floor according to a plot diagram. They can notice the rising and falling actions that contributes to the conflicts and resolution. The benefit of working in this way is that club members can each contribute to parts of the sticky note plot diagram, and students can remove and manipulate the sticky notes as they work together to reach a consensus. In Figure 5.22, you can see one club doing this work on a whiteboard, as they read *The Lightning Thief* by Rick Riordan.

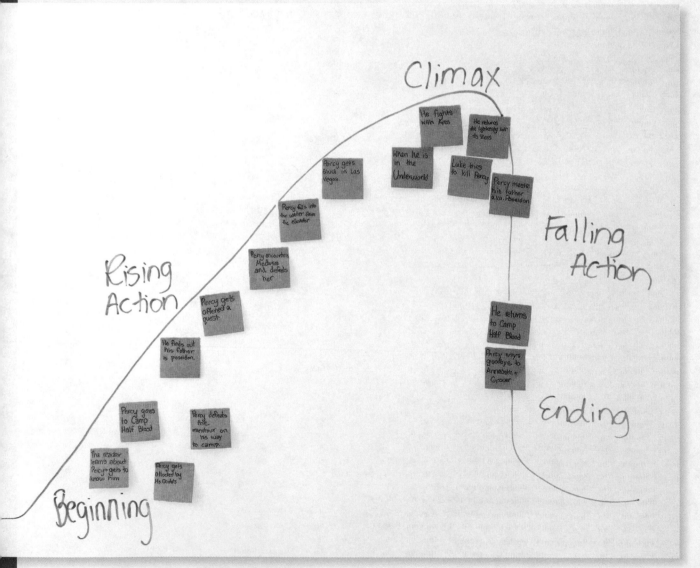

Figure 5.22 Sticky Note Plot Diagram

Finding Character Motivations

Pitfall: Club members are having difficulty identifying the characters' motivations. They are not asking questions pertaining to why the characters are making certain choices.

Pathway: A quick way to help get a book club or the whole class back on track is to have students identify the major choices and decisions of a main character in their book, and then ask themselves why.

Model this strategy first with a picture book, short text, or digital text. You may ask students to create a simple T-chart in their reader's notebooks or on a Google Doc. Figure 5.23 was created by fourth-grade students reading *Because of Winn-Dixie* by Kate DiCamillo. Students color-coded their responses. This work helps students step into the shoes of the characters, and empathize or critique their actions.

Characters' Actions/ Decisions	Why????
Opal lied about winn-dixie being her real dog.	Opal lied because she didn't want winn dixie to go to the pound. I think she wanted to keep Winn-Dixie because he smiled and answered to his name. She also loves animals. She knew the manager was angry and might send Winn dixie to the pound.

Figure 5.23 Google Doc T-Chart

6: Living with Books All Year Long

When our students enter their classrooms, they hope that each day is magical. Book clubs are wonder-filled worlds for our students' genuine engagement with reading. Dragons, sports heroes, and outer space are within reach, residing in the books students choose to read and discuss with their peers. Dr. Mary Howard tweeted, "We don't *teach* reading; we *inspire* readers by making room for opportunities that BECKON kids to live readerly lives in AND out of school" (2017). As teachers, this is our goal: for our students to live authentic, readerly lives. And we truly believe that book clubs are the spark that ignites an awakening in the hearts and minds of our students.

The pathway to students' growth as readers is long and ongoing; throughout this journey they will experience many successes. Recognizing their accomplishments inspires them to continue along the path. When we celebrate students' learning, this doesn't mark the end of book clubs. On the contrary, it opens the door for continued reading and discussions in future book club opportunities both in our classrooms and beyond them.

To commemorate a book club experience, we can provide a short window of time for collaborative student work that is reflective of their growth as readers. As full-time teachers, we know that finding time for book club projects is a luxury that many of us simply do not have. Truth be told, we'd rather our students use their time for additional reading. However, we can honor the work that has taken place during book clubs in ways that motivate students to do exactly that—continue a life of reading.

The wonderful book clubs that have been nurtured can continue beyond the four walls of our classrooms. Take Paulie, a third grader, who created a book club with nine of her friends during lunchtime because they just didn't want book clubs to end. Together, they read *The Lemonade War* by Jacqueline Davies and applied many of the strategies they learned from their teacher. And Max, an eighth grader, who started an online book club for his soccer team inspired by *Booked* by Kwame Alexander and *Tangerine* by Edward Bloor. Paulie and Max show us that there are many opportunities for book clubs to exist beyond the classroom. Some of these clubs might be part of a before- or after-school program at your school or they might be offered by a local library. Our goal is to continually demonstrate for students the joy and love of reading that exists not only in our classrooms, but in the world.

Celebrating Book Clubs: Inspiring Students to Read!

Book club celebrations can spotlight student growth in highly engaging ways that also strengthen comprehension and spur interest in reading. Whether you have one day or one week, here are some of our favorite ways to celebrate, and they can be customized to fit any schedule.

BOOK TALKS

Resource 6.1, p. 155

How often have you asked a friend, family member, or colleague for a good book recommendation? We ask the people we trust and whose opinions we value and respect. The same goes for our students. Invite your students to create dynamic book talks that help their classmates learn about the books they've read and loved. Encourage your clubs to "sell" their books to their peers. Book talks are short, and they can be delivered in front of the whole class or in small groups. Your students have seen you book talk during book clubs, and in this way you've modeled how to do this.

There are three simple steps to create a book talk:

1) Write a quick summary of the overall plot of the book.
2) Include a brief passage that will grab your listeners' attention.
3) Talk about what kinds of readers will enjoy this book. An example of this is, "If you are a reader who likes suspense and mystery, this is the book for you!"

For added fun, you might consider filming the book talks for your class website. Or you might ask students to post their book talks on your class blog. After a few years, you will have an extensive collection of book talks!

BOOK TRAILERS

Resource 6.2, p. 156

Whether we go out to the movies or watch from home, sometimes the best part of the experience is the movie trailers that precede. Action-packed and emotionally charged clips engage our senses and get us excited about what to see next. Many teachers use book trailers with parallel purpose: to get kids excited about what to read next!

Book trailers bring both fiction and nonfiction books and texts to life. They are visual representations of a book designed to interest potential readers. Technology continues to play an important role in book club celebrations as students explore a full range of remix possibilities using digital platforms and the text they've read to create a book trailer that promotes their book.

Figure 6.1 provides a QR code to a book talk on YouTube, and Figure 6.2 contains some tips that can help students create book trailers.

https://youtu.be/GcilWij2qnA

Figure 6.1
Book Trailer for *The Crazy Man*, by Pamela Porter

TRAILER TIPS	
Plan!	Use a storyboard to plan the format and order of your trailer. Which parts of the book will you feature? What images will you need to find? Collect the images. Save them as JPEGs in a folder that can be uploaded to Google Drive later.
Content!	Use literary elements to convey the storyline. Present parts of the book that help to show mood, setting, and theme. Pique interest without giving away too much of the book, particularly the end.
Software!	Select user-friendly software such as WeVideo, Photo Story 3, or Movie Maker. View a tutorial to understand how it works (for example, http://tinyurl.com/WeVideoBookTrailers).
Production!	Layout first! Once each scene is in place, then experiment with special effects such as music, movement, or color. Remember to focus on the purpose of this work. The trailer should persuade the audience to read the book! Use the cover of the book with the title and author. Select images and music that match (not distract from) the story. Speak clearly and at an appropriate pace during voice-overs.

Figure 6.2 Trailer Tips / Tech Tips

There is no one right way to make a book trailer. Many teachers develop a rubric with their students to identify the specific criteria they'd like book clubs to meet as they create their trailers. The creation of book trailers helps to broaden our students' understanding of literacies from a static, conventional, print-based conception to an appreciation of literacies as a shifting, evolving, and dynamic force.

INTERACTIVE BOOK POSTERS

Older students enjoy opportunities to apply their digital literacy skills to create an interactive book poster that persuades their peers to read a featured book club book. The purpose of this interactive poster is to engage peers'

Resource 6.3, p. 157

143

The 4 Bookateers Present:
Revolution by Deborah
Wiles

FREEDOM RIDERS

Freedom Summer

Revolution by Deborah Wiles takes place in June of 1964, the beginning of Freedom Summer. Freedom Summer was a protest movement to encourage Black people to vote. Volunteers of all races came down from the North to encourage black men and women to register to vote. Many believed that once Black people could vote, they could change the town they were living in. Although most protested peacefully, they were not met with the same kindness. There were shootings, many teargas uses, and beatings. Nevertheless, the freedom fighters persisted. In the book, Sunny sees in the newspaper that the "invaders" are coming down from the North. They are called invaders because there was many of them coming at one time, and they occupied the towns in the south. Although many White people were not welcoming, some families welcomed the newcomers into their homes. The freedom summer fighters were very brave, and they helped to change history. To learn more about Freedom Summer and about Freedom Riders scan these codes:

Segregation and Swimming Pools

Similar to the pool described in Revolution by Deborah Wiles, this swimming pool is segregated, available only to white people. In the story, people drained the water in a African-American pool. The only pool in town is now for white people only. Like many other pools in the Southern United States in the 1960's, African Americans were not included in many activities such as swimming in public pools. The Jim Crow laws stated that African Americans and whites were "separate, but equal". The novel proves that facilities influenced by the Jim Crow Laws were separate, but definitely not equal. Scan this QR code to learn how this discriminatory practice continues to affect African Americans today.

Figure 6.3 Interactive Book Poster

visual and auditory senses to promote a book that club members love (see Figure 6.3).

One way that club members can approach this work is to design their poster on one Google Slide. They can divide that one slide into however many different sections they'd like. For example, if there are four sections, they can choose four specific minitopics that will become the sections of their poster. Club members will decide upon the essential information to be included in each section as well as a key image that represents each minitopic. Minitopics can be literary elements, the characters from a multiple perspective novel, or events.

For example, students may decide that setting will be one of the minitopics of their poster. They can use an image that represents something about the setting of the book and develop a written response about how the setting of the book influences the characters. For fiction and nonfiction texts, the different sections can include images, interviews, maps, videos, songs, and so on. Students can generate a QR code for these digital texts that relate to the book for their peers to access via smart device. Remind students to include citations for all information, images, and sources used.

Once the layout, writing, and QR codes are complete, the poster can be printed on large paper. For students using Google, there are several easy-to-follow tutorials available online to guide this work. In Figure 6.4, sixth-grade students interact with the work of The 4 Bookateers book club, which read Revolution by Deborah Wiles.

Figure 6.4 Students Scanning QR Code on Interactive Book Poster

VISUAL VIGNETTES

In literature, a vignette is a short, descriptive scene or passage that zooms in on one particular moment to give an impression about a character, mood, or setting. We use the phrase *visual vignette* because rather than just discussing and writing about a passage from a text, students will act out a specific scene.

Resource 6.4, p. 158

Students love opportunities to act in class. During this process they get to move and express their interpretations of a text. Kinesthetic learning draws on movement, visuals, and story and allows students to collaborate and celebrate their book clubs.

Visual vignettes are particularly effective with students who have diverse learning styles since movement helps with focus and attention. Furthermore, the process of performing a text builds a bridge between the words on a page and the ideas they represent.

A visual vignette demonstrates how students have internalized the elements of literature and their interpretations of the text. Figure 6.5 is an example of the planning sheet and guiding questions seventh-grade members of the Reading Rockets book club used to create a visual vignette that they performed in class.

There are no specific rules for students to create visual vignettes, but it is important to give students options. However, unlike a tableau, which is a "living picture" where students freeze into a particular pose, there must be some action, not just reading the words of a text. This process encourages higher-level thinking skills as students visualize and connect with the words to convey them. Furthermore, rehearsals become an extension of previous book club discussions as they discover potential misunderstandings of a text and address them in a safe, low-risk, fun manner.

Text & Author - Which text have you and your club members chosen to work with? What type of text is this?	*"Early Autumn" by Langston Hughes* *Short story*
Content - Which part of the text will you portray? Why have you chosen this part? Is it the part that: • has the most energy? • left you wondering or puzzled? • troubled you the most? • has stayed with you long after reading? • revealed something to you?	*We'll be portraying the part where Bill and Mary run into each other in Washington Square park that revealed to us that Mary still loves Bill even after all these years.*
Style: How will you portray this part of the story? Will this be a linear portrayal of one part of the story or several short snapshots from the entire story?	*Linear*
Which literary elements will be demonstrated in your visual vignette? How will you portray these elements? • Characterization • Symbolism • Setting • Dialogue • Theme	*Characterization - One of us will be Bill and one of us will be Mary.* *Dialogue - We will say the words of each character in this scene.* *Setting - We have asked some peers to help us. They will sit on seats to pretend they're sitting on a bench in the park. Some will stand like trees in the park and slowly drop paper leaves from their hands.* *Symbolism - Autumn is a symbol so the trees fit this element. And 2 students will be the wind.*

Figure 6.5 Vignettes Graphic Organizer

Resources 6.5, p. 159,
and 6.6, p. 160

BOOK BISTRO

Literacy specialist Abbe Hocherman created an exciting way for students to celebrate their successes in book clubs. Book Bistro is an ongoing café-style structure designed to celebrate, share, and encourage reading. To culminate the end of a book club cycle, Book Bistro provides opportunities for students to learn about some of the texts their peers have read in other clubs. During Book Bistro, students continue to hone their skills as discussants of texts and implement reading comprehension strategies taught in book clubs and in reading workshop. Abbe recommends the following tips for organizing a Book Bistro:

1) Choose a Book Bistro date and let students know.

2) Prior to the Book Bistro date, students select one of the books they've read during book clubs. Members of a club do not all have to select the same text. Ask students to complete an "info card" so you know which book they intend to discuss at the Book Bistro.

3) With students, brainstorm different topics they can discuss and ways to engage their peers.

4) Once you've collected all of the cards, divide students into small Book Bistro groups. For this event, students have the opportunity to talk to and hear from peers outside of their book club. Group students in a variety of ways or ask students how they'd like to be grouped—by series, author, genre, protagonists of a certain type, or thematic connections, among others.

5) On the day of Book Bistro, students come prepared with their book, their engaging discussion plan, and an edible contribution to the Book Bistro café. For younger grades, teachers may want to collect students' books and discussion plans prior to the event to avoid forgotten work. Set up an area of the classroom for the edible contributions.

6) Before the Book Bistro begins, remind students about discussion goals. Teachers may want to display a Suggestions to Combat Common Pitfalls in Discussions chart for students to reference. Students grab snacks and disperse to their Book Bistro group to begin discussions!

7) Invite students to complete a brief recommendation information sheet with basic information about the book they've discussed such as title, author, genre, and a brief response to the question: What kind of reader would like this book? These sheets can be kept in a classroom binder titled What to Read Next! so that all students have access to recommendations from their peers.

Book Bistro creates opportunities for students to decide how to begin and sustain conversations about the great books they've read. It is their time to talk and enjoy the books and discussions in a genuine way and to leave with ideas for the next book they want to read. For students, Book Bistro is a book club party or celebration, not an assignment.

Book Clubs Beyond the Classroom

Our primary goal as teachers of reading is to inspire our students to become independent, lifelong readers. We discussed the ways in which book clubs can reside in your classroom; however, if we truly want our students to become lifelong readers, we need to provide pathways for them to take book clubs beyond the classroom. We can create these pathways by supporting optional book clubs that meet outside the reading/literacy block. These clubs can meet before, during, and after school hours. They can meet once a week, month, or quarter. The best part about these book clubs is how easy it is to customize them to fit the needs of your school community and students. Joan Slattery, sixth- through twelfth-grade librarian, reflects on the impact of book clubs beyond the classroom. "A vibrant and visible school book club fuels a culture of reading beyond the club itself. Even among students who don't choose to join. We see increased interest in popular book club books among *all* students as posters go up, club announcements are made, book buzz spreads. Word of mouth from student to student is the best book promotion, hands down." As Joan explains, "book buzz" helps to "fuel a culture of reading" that spreads far beyond classrooms and clubs themselves. Reading becomes a staple in our students' everyday lives.

MOCK NEWBERY BOOK CLUB / MOCK CALDECOTT CLUB

The American Library Association Awards (ALA) are presented each year at the midwinter meeting. There are many book awards including: The Coretta Scott King Award, the Pura Belpré Award, the Newbery Medal, and the Caldecott Medal. You can create a "Mock Newbery Club" or a "Mock Caldecott Club" for the students in your school. In fact, there are many clubs like these at public libraries around the country.

Resource 6.7, p. 161

Dana, along with her colleagues Maureen Corbo and Joan Slattery, co-lead the fifth- and sixth-grade Mock Newbery Club at their school. Students read the books that were published during the year and weigh in on whether they believe the books should earn the Newbery Medal. The teachers who run the club select six to eight options for their students to read each month. The club provides new dynamic texts that range in length. These can include graphic novels, picture books, and chapter books. Students can elect to read all the titles or pick one or two. At subsequent club meetings, students share their personal reactions, compare and contrast books, and offer each other recommendations. It's a raucous time filled with laughter, discussion, and listening.

Whether you have a Mock Newbery club or a Mock Caldecott club, you want to make sure that your students have the chance to vote for their favorite book of the year. Students can also vote for awards such as "Best Character," "Most Suspenseful Storyline," "Favorite Cover," and so on. For the ultimate celebration, students and teachers can tune into the ALA Awards Show live. It is streamed on the ALA website and usually happens in January or February. The ALA awards show can also be viewed at a later date on the ALA website. To find out more about the ALA Youth Media Awards, visit www.ala.org. Joan Slattery says, "Streaming it live for our entire fifth and sixth grades creates a sense of excitement around these 'Academy Awards' of children's literature. The students are thrilled to simply recognize a cover, title, or author—even if they haven't read the book. They actually hold hands in anticipation, and then scream. It's something to see!"

ALL-SCHOOL AND GRADE-LEVEL BOOK CLUBS

To develop a strong community of readers, you can work with your colleagues to create an all-school book club. We know educators who have created book clubs for their high school or middle school by selecting texts that are appropriate for all ages in the school to read. These are optional book clubs that generally meet before school hours, during lunches, after school, or even virtually over winter or summer break. These clubs are a terrific opportunity for students who want to be part of a community of readers from different grade levels. For all-school reads, students have opportunities to discuss books with peers from different grade levels.

Grade-level book clubs allow students from various classes to come together and hear each other's ideas about books. For instance, there might be three or four different sections of seventh-grade language arts in a school; however, all seventh-grade students can join a book club that meets during lunch once a month to discuss a common text.

What's powerful about all-school and grade-level book clubs is the opportunity to amplify the voices of many students in a book club experience. Additionally, these experiences foster a culture of reading.

IDENTITY AND INTEREST GROUP BOOK CLUBS

Many book clubs serve as identity and interest groups for students, and these clubs are run by librarians and educators who are passionate about a variety of topics. For instance, there are identity book clubs that include students who identify with a specific gender. Educators have found that it can be challenging sometimes to draw boys into book clubs, so they've created all-boy clubs. These clubs read texts that are selected by their club members to promote reading among boys. Likewise, all-girl book clubs allow girls to discuss issues that are important to them and may not be discussed in the classroom. Identity book clubs have also become safe havens for students who feel marginalized in their schools and in the world. For example, there are book clubs specifically for African American boys and for LGBTQ+ youth. They can read about and discuss issues that are reflective of their lives.

Interest book clubs can also create spaces for students to read texts that appeal to them and are often underrepresented in the literacy curricula. These book clubs might be The Graphic Novel Club, Books That Cook, The Comic Book Club, The Coding Book Club, or The Animal Lovers Book Club, among others.

Identity and interest book clubs are spaces that truly value what's in the hearts and minds of students and provide opportunities for them to develop and explore their reading identities.

JANE ADDAMS BOOK CLUB

The Jane Addams Children's Book Award is given each October at the United Nations in New York City to authors and illustrators whose work focuses on social justice. These books address a variety of issues and topics such as racism, sexism, heteronormativity, prejudice, war, classism, and ableism. Examples of books that have received this prestigious award are *Steamboat School,* by Deborah Hopkinson and illustrated by Ron Husband; *We Will Not Be Silent: The White Rose Student Resistance Movement That Defied Adolf Hitler,* by Russell Freedman; and *Full Cicada Moon,* by Marilyn Hilton.

For students and educators interested in social justice book clubs, a great place to start is to visit the Jane Addams website (http://www.janeaddamschildrensbookaward.org/) to review the titles of powerful picture books, novels, and informational books. For many years, Sonja served as a Jane Addams Children's Book Award Committee member. She and her colleague and friend Michelle Kaczmarek facilitated The Jane Addams Children's Literature Circle for Girls. These book clubs were composed of five to six girls who began reading together outside of school in sixth grade and into their high school years. The club met once a month at the home of one of the girls. With Sonja and Michelle's support, the girls engaged in emotional conversations about characters, people, events, and the injustices demonstrated in the texts.

Social justice–themed book clubs are opportunities for students to engage in further conversations beyond the classroom. In social justice book clubs, kids get to delve deep into issues they care about the most.

FAMILY/FRIEND–STUDENT BOOK CLUBS

Family/friend–student book clubs are a great way to get family members or friends to foster a child's love of reading. There are two different options for this type of club. Clubs can be held at the end of the school day, or you can encourage family members or friends to have a club meeting at home.

For example, if you are a fifth-grade teacher, you might include *Wonder* by R. J. Palacio as your first title. You can invite family or friends into school so they can discuss the book with other guests and students in small groups. Or, if the club is meeting at home, the book can be discussed there. If you choose the latter option, you might consider sending home a list of potential book club questions that will ignite a meaningful discussion.

Engaging family and friends in your literacy curriculum is a powerful way to promote reading. When the people who love and care for your students take an interest in reading and talking about books, students see role models at home and in their community.

SUMMER BOOK CLUBS

We all strive to ensure that our students read over the summer. We know, all too well, the reading gains that students can make or lose during the summer months. Studies have shown that when students read during the summer, they remain on grade level or advance. Kylene Beers, author of *Notice and Note* (Beers and Probst 2012), writes,

> Summer reading isn't about reading a certain number of titles from a list someone else has compiled. It's not about finishing *A Tale of Two Cities* before the first day of tenth grade. It's not about reading books at a certain Lexile level or AR level. It's not about preparing for a test, keeping a dialectical journal to be submitted, or logging a certain number of hours or titles in a journal that will eventually be graded. Summer reading is about holding a book in your hands. . . . Summer reading is about kicking off your shoes, staying up much too late, reading all day with no one caring that's what you're doing. It's about rushing through one [book] to get to the next or lingering as long as you want. (Beers 2005)

Kylene's words resonate in our minds as we think about summer book clubs being a joyful reading experience.

Summer book clubs can be a continuation of the clubs you have in your classroom, or students can elect to create new clubs with their peers, neighbors, or campmates. Summer book clubs are student driven and require little teacher support. We've found that all it takes is saying to our class at the end of the school year, "Book clubs do not need to end. They can continue during the summertime. Perhaps this is something your club is interested in, or maybe you'd like to form a new book club with friends, neighbors, family members, or camp friends." Students can usually run with the idea from there. We've seen book clubs flourish over the summer, as friends get together or text each other their thoughts about books.

TEACHER BOOK CLUBS

The best advice we have for teachers who are using book clubs is to also participate in an adult book club. One of the most valuable pieces of advice that Lucy Calkins has shared with us is: If you are a teacher of reading, you too need to read. If you are a teacher of writing, you too need to write. We carry this advice with us each day. Whether you engage in an online book club community or physically meet together with a club, joining an adult book club is a must for teachers who want their students to be in book clubs.

Joining a teacher book club is the perfect way to practice what you preach and read, read, read. You might want to join an online teacher book club such as Donalyn Miller's #bookaday summer reading challenge, #titletalk, Oprah's Book Club, or Nerdy Book Club, among others. Or you can create a teacher book club at your school. This might look like a whole-school teacher book club, a departmental book club, or a grade-level teacher book club. This is a wonderful way to talk with your colleagues about books. For example, the teachers in your science department might get together and decide to read a book about a particular topic or pedagogy. Or, you might be a team of fourth-grade teachers who are determined to read one new children's chapter book a month, so you can book talk these new texts to your class. Or perhaps you have a group of teachers who wants to read the latest books on the *New York Times* bestseller list.

By engaging in book clubs, we act as reading role models for our students, and we can demonstrate the joy and love of reading that exists in the world.

Onward! Breathing New Life into Book Clubs

Building a community of lifelong, joyful readers is our central goal. Lifelong readers thrive independently in texts. They cultivate their interests and enhance their understanding of the world around them. In book clubs, students construct and reconstruct their reading identities. Creating authentic spaces for discussion and choice allows students to take risks and learn alongside others. This is the joyful learning we want to see in our classrooms.

As you forge ahead, we offer you three mantras for cultivating successful book clubs with students:

1) "Be Brave! Let Go! Pull Back!" As students journey through book clubs with peers, give them choice and ownership over their clubs. This will deepen their book club experience, and you will see them rise to the occasion.

2) "Embrace Authentic Discussions!" Trust that your students' conversations will improve over time—that they will grow and develop. Allow book clubs to have authentic discussions that ebb and flow as students become strong, independent discussants.

3) "Joy! Joy! Joy!" Joyful readers are lifelong readers. When students experience heartening reading experiences, they will want to read more. Build joyful reading communities by providing high-interest texts, helping clubs form strong identities, and encouraging students to read together.

The research shows that it is urgent that we act now. We must be unyielding in the goal of cultivating lifelong readers. Each one of us can take part in a reading revolution by breathing new life into book clubs. Each one of us can provide pathways that nurture a love of reading in our students.

Chapter Six Resources at a Glance

IDEAS	SPECIFICS	RESOURCES
Commemorate book club experiences! Spotlight student growth in ways that inspire additional reading.	*How can I celebrate students' reading achievements?* Invite book clubs to collaborate on one of the following projects: • Book talks • Book trailers • Interactive book poster • Visual vignette	**Resource 6.1: Planning a Book Talk** p. 155 **Resource 6.2: Storyboarding a Book Trailer** p. 156 **Resource 6.3: Designing an Interactive Poster** p. 157 **Resource 6.4: Visualizing a Vignette** p. 158
Plan a Book Bistro! Implement a café-style celebration of great books and great reading.	*How can I provide opportunities for students to discuss their reading and achievements with peers beyond their individual clubs?* Make new groupings to provide students with opportunities to talk to and hear from other peers about books they love. Group by: • Series • Author • Genre • Protagonist characteristics • Thematic connection	**Resource 6.5: Book Bistro Information Card** p. 159 **Resource 6.6: What to Read Next! Book Bistro Sheet** p. 160
Encourage book clubs beyond the classroom! Fuel a culture of reading that spreads beyond classrooms and clubs.	*How can I help reading to become a staple in the everyday lives of my students?* Create pathways for book clubs beyond the classroom such as: • Mock Newbery book clubs • Mock Caldecott book clubs • All-school and grade-level book clubs • Identity book clubs • Interest group book clubs • Jane Addams book club • Parent-student book clubs • Summer book clubs	**Resource 6.7: Voting Sheet for Mock Newbery / Mock Caldecott Clubs** p. 161

PATHWAY RESOURCES

To download and print digital versions of the reproducible forms found in this book, visit the online resources at **http://heinpub/newlifebookclubs-login**. Enter your email address and password (or click "Create New Account" to set up an account). Once you have logged in, enter keycode **NULIFE** and click "Register."

Planning a Book Talk

BOOK TALKS THAT ROCK!

Read any great books lately? Of course you have! Tell us about it! Here's how:

Summary Write a *quick* summary of the overall plot of the book. Include the title of the book and the author. • Who are the main characters and what are they like? • Where and when does this story take place? • What is the main problem/conflict? • What is a central theme of the story? **Remember not to give away the ending!**	
Passage Include a *brief* passage that will grab the attention of your peers. Consider a part that: • Made you laugh out loud • Caused you to marvel at the imagery • Shows tension • Left you wondering	**Flag this passage in your book with a sticky note**.
Why *this* book? Talk about what kinds of readers will enjoy this book. An example of this is, "If you are a reader who likes suspense and mystery, this is the book for you!"	

6.2 Storyboarding a Book Trailer

Name: _____ **Date:** _____

Book Title: _____

Author's Name: _____

Directions: To create your book trailer, use the storyboard below to think about what each slide in your trailer will include. Be sure to think about images, quotes from the book, music, and possibly narration (your voice).

Designing an Interactive Poster

6.3

INSTRUCTIONS

Step 1:   Open Google Slides. You'll only need one slide to design your poster.

Step 2:   Include the title and author of the book and the name of your book club.

Step 3:   Create four or five specific "minitopics" from the reading that will become sections on your poster. Minitopics can be literary elements, main characters, or specific events, among others.

Step 4:   Determine the essential information and key images to be included in each section.

Step 5:   Generate a QR code that when accessed via smartphone or another device provides additional information (images, interviews, maps, videos, music, etc.) about each minitopic.

Step 6:   Review and proofread your work before printing on large paper.

Tip: There are online tutorials for creating posters from various digital platforms, such as Google, that you can refer to.

6.4 Visualizing a Vignette

Text and Author—Which text have you and your club members chosen to work with? What type of text is this?	
Content—Which part of the text will you portray? Why have you chosen this part? • Does the part have the most energy? • Did it leave you wondering or puzzled? • Did it trouble you the most? • Has it stayed with you long after reading? • Has it revealed something to you?	
Style—How will you portray this part of the story? Will this be a linear portrayal of one part of the story or several short snapshots from the entire story?	
Which literary elements will be demonstrated in your visual vignette? How will you portray these elements? • Characterization • Symbolism • Setting • Dialogue • Theme	

Book Bistro Information Card

Name: _____ Date: _____

Book Title: _____ Genre: _____

Author's Name: _____

Topics I plan to discuss:

1.

2.

3.

Plans for engaging my peers:

6.6   **What to Read Next! Book Bistro Sheet**

Title: _____

Author: _____   **Genre:** _____

What kind of reader would like this book?

Recommender:

Voting Sheet for Mock Newbery / Mock Caldecott Clubs

Book most likely to win the Newbery Medal	Book most likely to win the Caldecott Medal	Book with the *best* cover
Book with the *best* main character	**Book with the *best* villain**	**Funniest book**
Most heartwarming book	**Most original plot**	**Most memorable character**

References

Ahmed, Sara K. 2018. *Being The Change*. Portsmouth, NH: Heinemann.

Allington, Richard L. 2012. *What Really Matters for Struggling Readers: Designing Research-Based Programs*. 3rd ed. Boston: Pearson.

Atwell, Nancie. 1987. *In the Middle: A Lifetime of Learning About Writing, Reading, and Adolescents*. Portsmouth, NH: Heinemann.

Beers, Kylene. 2005. "Four Guidelines for Summer Reading." http://kylenebeers .com/blog/2014/05/04/guidelines-for-summer-reading/.

Beers, Kylene, and Robert E. Probst. 2012. *Notice and Note*: *Strategies for Close Reading*. Portsmouth, NH: Heinemann.

Bomer, Katherine. 2010. *Hidden Gems: Naming and Teaching from the Brilliance in Every Students' Writing*. Portsmouth, NH: Heinemann.

Bradley, Kimberly Brubaker. 2016. *The War That Saved My Life*. New York: Puffin Books.

BrainyQuote. n.d. "Beyonce Knowles Quotes." https://www.brainyquote.com /quotes/beyonce_knowles_596349.

Calkins, Lucy. 2010. *Guide to the Reading Workshop: Grades 3–5*. Portsmouth, NH: Heinemann.

Candlewick Press. 2016. "Raymie Nightingale by Kate Di Camillo Book Trailer." https://youtu.be/65ByjC7v_EE.

Cherry-Paul, Sonja, and Dana Johansen. 2014. *Teaching Interpretation: Using Text-Based Evidence to Construct Meaning*. Portsmouth, NH: Heinemann.

de la Peña, Matt. 2018. Closing Workshop at Summer Writing Institute. Lecture presented at Teachers College Reading Writing Project, Teachers College, Columbia University, New York, June 20.

DuPrau, Jeanne. 2003. *The City of Ember*. New York: Random House Children's Books.

Fountas and Pinnell. Twitter post. January 25, 2018, 5:23 PM. https://twitter .com/fountaspinnell/status/956699129350107142?lang=en.

Freire, Paulo. 1970. *Pedagogy of the Oppressed*. New York: Herder and Herder.

harperteen. 2011. "*Divergent* by Veronica Roth—Book Trailer." https://youtu.be /tu5Erw-posg.

Howard, Jacqueline. 2017. "Report: Young Kids Spend over 2 Hours a Day on Screens." CNN. October 19. https://www.cnn.com/2017/10/19/health /children-smartphone-tablet-use-report/index.html.

Howard, Dr. Mary. Twitter Post. June 7, 2017, 12:05 PM. https://twitter.com /DrMaryHoward/status/872530018139856903.

Kamenetz, Anya. 2017. "Young Children Are Spending Much More Time in Front of Small Screens." NPR. October 19. https://www.npr.org/sections/ed/2017/10/19/558178851/young-children-are-spending-much-more-time-in-front-of-small-screens.

Left Bank Books. 2016. "Jason Reynolds: Why It's Important for Kids to Read." https://www.youtube.com/watch?v=ATeoup5a-XU&feature=youtu.be.

Miller, Donalyn. 2009. *The Book Whisperer: Awakening the Inner Reader in Every Child.* San Francisco: Jossey-Bass.

———. 2017. "Girl Characters Are Human Characters: Empowering Girls and Boy Readers Through Strong Female Characters." Lecture presented at International Literacy Association Conference, Orlando, FL, July 16.

Mulligan, Tammy, and Clare Landrigan. 2018. *It's All About the Books: How to Create Bookrooms and Classroom Libraries.* Portsmouth, NH: Heinemann.

National Center for Education Statistics. 2015. *National Assessment of Educational Progress.* Washington, DC: U.S. Department of Education.

———. 2018. *National Assessment of Educational Progress.* Washington, DC: U.S. Department of Education.

National Endowment for the Arts. 2007. "To Read or Not to Read: A Question of National Consequence." Research Division Report No. 47. https://www.arts.gov/sites/default/files/ToRead.pdf.

Park, Linda Sue. 2010. *A Long Walk to Water.* New York: Clarion Books.

Penguin Middle School. 2018. "Jacqueline Woodson's New Book *Harbor Me.*" https://www.youtube.com/watch?v=FjKqwqpBgGM.

Porter, Pamela. 2005. *The Crazy Man.* Toronto, ON: Groundwood Books.

Pranikoff, Kara. 2017. *Teaching Talk. A Practical Guide to Fostering Student Thinking and Conversation.* Portsmouth, NH: Heinemann.

Reading Rockets. 2014. "Transcript from an Interview with Jacqueline Woodson." http://www.readingrockets.org/books/interviews/woodson/transcript.

readwritethink. n.d. "MyTube: Make a Video Public Service Announcement." http://www.readwritethink.org/parent-afterschool-resources/activities-projects/mytube-make-video-public-30157.html.

Rich, Adrienne. 1994. *Blood, Bread, and Poetry: Selected Prose, 1979–1985.* New York: W. W. Norton & Company.

Ripp, Pernille. 2017. *Passionate Readers: The Art of Reaching and Engaging Every Child.* New York: Routledge.

Roberts, Kate. 2018. *A Novel Approach.* Portsmouth, NH: Heinemann.

Research Studies on Book Clubs

Barone, Diane. 2011. "Making Meaning: Individual and Group Response Within a Book Club Structure." *Journal of Early Childhood Literacy* 13 [1]: 3–25.

Broughton, Mary. 2002. "The Performance and Construction of Subjectivities of Early Adolescent Girls in Book Club Discussions." *Journal of Literacy Research* 34 [1]: 1–38.

Casey, Heather K. 2009. "Engaging the Disengaged: Using Learning Clubs to Motivate Struggling Adolescent Readers and Writers." *Journal of Adolescent & Adult Literacy* 52 (4): 284–94.

Denyer, Jenny, and Debra LaFleur. 2001. "The Eliot Conference: An Analysis of a Peer Response Group." *Voices from the Middle* 9 (1): 29–39.

Dias-Mitchell, Laurie, and Elizabeth Harris. 2001. "Multicultural Mosaic: A Family Book Club." *Knowledge Quest* 29 (4): 17–21.

Hill, K. Dara. 2008. "Conflict in a Sixth-Grade Book Club: The Impact of a Rule-Driven Discourse." *Voices from the Middle* 16 (2): 16–24.

Hoffman, A. Robin. 2010. "The BFG and the Spaghetti Book Club: A Case Study of Children as Critics." *Children's Literature in Education* 41 (3): 234–50.

Kimasi, Kafi. 2014. "Connected Learning: Linking Academics, Popular Culture, and Digital Literacy in a Young Urban Scholars Book Club." *Teacher Librarian* 41 (3): 8–15.

Lapp, Diane, and Douglas Fisher. 2009. "It's All About the Book: Motivating Teens to Read." *Journal of Adolescent & Adult Literacy* 52 (7): 556–61.

Paxton-Buursma, Debra, and Melodee Walker. 2008. "Piggybacking: A Strategy to Increase Participation in Classroom Discussions by Students with Learning Disabilities." *Council for Exceptional Children* 40 (3): 28–34.

Raphael, Taffy E., and Susan I. McMahon. 1994. "Book Club: An Alternative Framework for Reading Instruction." *The Reading Teacher* 48 (2): 102–16.

Seyfried, Jonathan. 2008. "Reinventing the Book Club." *Knowledge Quest* 36 (3): 44–48.

Shantz-Keresztes, Linda. 2005. "Wired for Words' On-line Youth Book Clubs." *School Libraries of Canada* 25 (1): 48–54.

Smith, Sally A. 2000. "Talking About 'Real Stuff': Explorations of Agency and Romance in an All-Girls' Book Club." *Language Arts* 78 (1): 30–38.

Taber, Nancy, Vera Woloshyn, and Laura Lane. 2012. "Food Chains, Frenemies, and Revenge Fantasies: Relating Fiction to Life in a Girls' Book Club." *Brock Education* 22 (1): 41–55.

Weih, Timothy G. 2008. "A Book Club Sheds Light on Boys and Reading." *Middle School Journal* 40 (1): 19–25.

Whittingham, Jeff, and Stephanie Huffman. 2009. *Reading Improvement* 46 (3): 130–36.

Zambo, Debby, and Carey Hansen. 2013. "Using Literacy to Understand Mexican Boys' Perspectives of Life." *Association of Mexican-American Educators Journal* 7 (1): 48–57.